PRAYING FOR

GOD'S PRESENCE IN

This Marriage

Tamela and Bill Barden
(Given to)

as they reaffirm their wedding vows
(On the Occasion of)

December 13th, 2008
(Date)

from Al & Margaret Heston
(From)

with congratulations for the marriage
you've had and our prayers for a
greater one to come!

LORD, BLESS THIS MARRIAGE

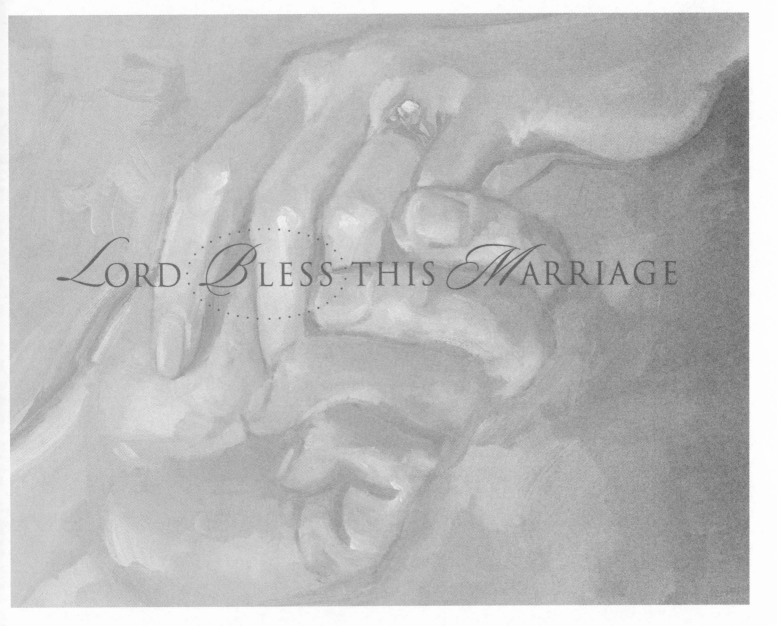

LORD BLESS THIS MARRIAGE

WILLIAM & NANCIE CARMICHAEL

TYNDALE HOUSE PUBLISHERS, INC. WHEATON, ILLINOIS

Visit Tyndale's exciting Web site at www.tyndale.com

Healthy Home Books are designed to strengthen marriages and families by helping to create a home environment that nourishes relationships, builds character, models sound values, and encourages spiritual growth. A Healthy Home—it's what we all desire for ourselves and our children.

Designed by Jackie Noe

Edited by Lynn Vanderzalm

Library of Congress Catalogue-in-Publication Data
Carmichael, William, date
  Lord, bless this marriage : a keepsake prayer journal to pray for the presence of God in your marriage / William and Nancie Carmichael.
    p. cm.
  ISBN 0-8423-3855-1 (alk. paper)
  1. Spouses—Prayer-books and devotions—English. 2. Marriage—Religious aspects—Christianity. 3. Spiritual journals—Authorship. I. Carmichael, Nancie. II. Title.
BV4596.M3C37 1999
242′.644—dc21   98-31854

Printed in the United States of America.

05 04 03 02 01 00 99
 8   7   6   5   4   3   2   1

CONTENTS

ACKNOWLEDGMENTS

Hundreds of people helped us with this book. Thanks to all of you who filled out the questionnaires and surveys with very helpful and candid insights. Special thanks to our dear friends, who gave us valuable brainstorming and feedback, including Steve and Cindy, Pat and Connie, Ned and Celesté, Wayne and Connie, Gene and Marylou, Rich and June, Marty and Betsy, Bob and Joan, and so many more.

Thanks also to Celesté Clements, who did a good job of helping us find many of the quotations, and to our wonderful editor, Lynn Vanderzalm, who always seems to know how to make something read so much better.

When Bill and I first began seriously dating, it was easy to pray together. We both wanted God's will for our lives, and it seemed natural to pray. Then after we got married and the years went by, we found that we didn't pray together as often as we had earlier in our marriage. In our busy lives, it's easy for us not to take time to pray together. Bill likes to go to sleep at ten o'clock on the dot. I'm ready to talk then. Bill is up bright and early, and I don't even believe in God until nine o'clock and I've had two cups of coffee (just kidding)!

But we also suspect that the real reason we don't pray together is because of what's going on inside us. When we enter God's presence, we can't play games. We must lay down our defenses, be transparent and open with one another. When we pray together, we cannot avoid important issues. We must deal with them, or our hearts could harden toward one another.

We're not the only ones who find praying together as a couple a challenge. Before we started writing this book, we sent surveys to over 250 couples, asking them about their prayer lives. Almost all of the couples who responded to the survey said they wanted to improve their prayer lives together. But many of them also indicated that praying together was hard for them. Some indicated that they had a hard time finding the time. Others just found it awkward. Diana told us, "We prayed together once, but my husband likes to pray to the Lord quietly, by himself." Julie and Rick, married nineteen years, told us that when they learned to pray together, they felt a sense of oneness they never dreamed they could have. They said, "It was a turning point because we realized that prayer was our source of strength."

We are excited about sharing this book about how to pray as a couple because something unusual and wonderful is happening in our own marriage. We're still the same people, with the same old vulnerabilities. But after more than thirty years of marriage, we see a strong, intangible *something* in our marriage that is new and precious.

What's different is that we *have been praying for the presence of God in specific areas of our marriage.* Prayer is powerful. It invokes the presence of God. And when we ask God to be present in our marriage, He comes, delighted at our invitation. Why should we be surprised? And why should we be surprised that the obstacles and hindrances to prayer are enormous? The enemy of our souls knows the powerful things that can happen in our marriages when we invite God's presence.

It's never too late to begin praying together. After thirty-five years of marriage, Elaine and Ken decided that prayer together was a lacking component in their lives. Through Ken's urging and leadership, they now make prayer a daily part of their lives. They declare, "It's been a lifeline."

Why Is It So Difficult to Pray Together?

Nancie and I were surprised to learn from our marriage survey that most couples find it harder to pray *together* than to pray alone. Praying with our spouse for our children is different from praying together for our marriage or other things. As parents, we have a natural nurturing response that makes praying for our children seem a natural part of parenting. But praying with our spouse for each other is different. Somehow we resist prayer within marriage. Perhaps it's because there can be overtones of authority and spiritual superiority within prayer. Perhaps it's due to unresolved conflict or lingering hurts. Perhaps it's a fear of being vulnerable. We eat together, sleep together, have sexual relations, share financial resources, have children together, make life plans together. These are truly intimate and vulnerable places. But in marriage we can also hurt one another most deeply because of the intimacy of the relationship. Most of us tend to keep very good accounts of who owes what to whom. The resistance to praying together can come from an attitude that says, "But you hurt me, and you owe me an apology" or "How can you expect me to pray with you when you owe me?" or "Until you pay, we can't pray." Forgiveness must be at the heart of our marriage relationships. Colossians 3:13 encourages us, "You must make allowance for each other's faults and forgive the person who offends you. Remember, the Lord forgave you, so you must forgive others."

If we can break down these walls of human resistance, a powerful strength and unity is formed when we pray together. It is a unity that binds not only a married couple to each other but also the Spirit of God to us. "A triple-braided cord is not easily broken" (Eccles. 4:12).

Another reason some couples find it hard to pray together is that their expectations are too high. When one spouse tends toward perfectionism (or when both spouses do, as is the case with Nancie and me), prayer is more challenging. Perfectionism can be a form of legalism; nothing is ever good enough, holy enough. Let's face it—perfectionism goes directly against grace and can build up barriers and walls within marriage.

Why Pray for Our Marriages?

As all married couples know, nothing exposes the heart, soul, mind, and body as marriage does. This most complex and challenging of relationships is a picture of God's love for His bride, His people. We are a metaphor of His love—of the longing, the seeking, the pursuing, the commitment. It only makes sense that we should invite His presence into our marriages. No other relationship brings us quite so much fulfillment and joy—or quite so much pain and disappointment. Frankly, we pray because we *need* His presence in our marriage.

It is a relief to know that Jesus has told us that in heaven we will not have our relationships clouded or complicated by need, drive, desire, and expectations. Our relationships will be love perfected. But while we live on earth, love is often hard work. We are housed within bodies that have their own agendas and emotional complexities. Our marriages are pressed by cultural and family expectations. If we are honest, we admit that the only way we are going to survive or thrive in our marriages is if we ask God to be present in and to rule in our relationship.

How Do We Find the Time and Place to Pray?

Some couples don't pray together because it's hard for them to get started, to find a time and place to pray together.

In Fritz Ridenour's book *The Marriage Collection,* Charlie and Martha Shedd wrote about their struggles in finding how to pray together in the early years of their marriage. Charlie wrote, "We decided on one more try. Only this time we would not give up. . . . This time we would study prayer. This time we would dig deep in the writings on prayer. We would begin again and keep on beginning and pray for a major break-through. Suddenly there it was—a new approach. Why not start our prayer time with the list of things we'd like to pray about? Then when we had shared enough to understand each other, we would go to the Lord together in silence.

"So that's how we did it. We would sit on our rocking love seat. We would take turns telling each other things we'd like to pray about. Then, holding hands, we would pray, each in our own way, silently. This was the beginning of prayer together that lasted [forty-seven years]. . . . We've learned to pray in every possible way, including aloud. Anytime, anywhere, every position, every setting, in everyday language. . . . Together we tune our friendship to the Friend of friends."

The Shedds found a style that worked for them. As you explore what will work for you, keep these things in mind.

Start where you are. If a simple prayer at a mealtime is a first step for you, start there. Suggest taking turns praying at mealtimes, and include praying about specific needs. This helps bring an awareness of God into your everyday life. You could also start by agreeing on what to pray for during that day or week, then pray separately and compare notes later.

Look for opportunities to pray. We have friends who believe strongly in the power of prayer and who are sensitive to opportunities to pray with others. When we are with them, we often end up praying together because someone will suggest, "Let's pray." These friends have modeled for us that in a nonthreatening atmosphere prayer can be a powerful bond.

Pray for God to give you the sensitivity to know when to pray with your spouse. Pray for your spouse when he or she is going through a difficult time. Pray when he or she has experienced God's guidance or peace or victory.

Agree on a time and place. As our children got older, "quiet time" at our house was in the morning. We continue that pattern even though our children are nearly out of the nest. We sit in the kitchen with a cup of coffee, share Scripture, and pray together. We try to be consistent yet not legalistic, making allowances for schedules. It's important not to give up or get down on ourselves if it isn't *just so.* We've also added other prayer times. We find that we like to pray together before we go to sleep. Some of our best and most concentrated prayer times are when we are on a trip together somewhere.

View your marriage as a third person in the relationship. It helps in praying for our marriage to see the marriage as a "third entity" that needs nurturing, protection, and love. There's the husband, the wife, and then us "as a couple." Respect and guard your relationship by praying for it. Nurture it, take care of it, and give it its own space.

What If My Spouse Doesn't Want to Pray with Me?

What if one person desires to pray within the marriage but his or her spouse does not? Tread carefully when approaching the subject of prayer with your spouse. It requires patience and discernment. A heavy-handed or insistent approach will only further harden the other's heart toward praying together.

You might start with a confession of personal need: "I really need God to help me in [name the situation or area of your life]. Would you be willing to pray for me during your quiet time about this?" By showing your own vulnerability first and confessing your own need, you are approaching your spouse in a non-defensive way. If you start with the question, "Is there anything I can pray about for you today?" your spouse may misunderstand and hear your question as, "I know you have a lot of needs [flaws or problems], so confess them, and I'll pray." Start by asking your spouse to pray for you. If your spouse says yes and is open to praying for you, then you might ask what he or she would like you to pray about.

Of course, if your spouse is not a believer, you need to start at the beginning. Continue to pray on your own and include consistent intercession for the salvation of your spouse. Don't give up. Praying for an unsaved spouse can be like a marathon run. It may be long and arduous business. Things may get worse before they get better. While God does not promise us that the answer will come on our time schedule, He does promise that our prayers are effective and will make a difference. Don't give up!

Pray for Each Other

Praying together as a couple begins with praying *for* one another. We have noticed that our love for each other has increased as we have learned to pray for each other. It increases our compassion and our sensitivity toward one another. As Patrick Morley wrote in *Two-Part Harmony,* "It is easier to pray *for* each other than it is to pray *with* each other. To pray with each other is a brave step toward intimacy. If you find it difficult, you are not alone. To share our prayers to the Almighty God with another person is to let him or her view the most personal aspect of our life. . . .

"When we pray for each other, the attitude of our own heart becomes softer and more forgiving toward our mate. It is impossible to earnestly pray for someone and be filled with hatred for them at the same time. If we will start to pray, even if angry, the Lord will give us peace. As you pray for your partner, you will find yourself letting go of your animosities, your reservations, your pettiness, and your insistence upon having your own way."

Pray with Each Other

When you do pray aloud together, keep in mind that you don't have to pray an eloquent prayer or something that would rival the prayer of St. Francis of Assisi. Simplicity and honesty are the key elements. You cannot pretend spirituality within a marriage because you know one another too well. Last night before Bill and I went to sleep, we were very tired. Bill grabbed my hand, and his prayer was simply, "Lord, thank You for this day." And I said, "Amen." And that was our prayer time for that night, but it was heartfelt and real. (And we know God understood!) Other times our prayers are more sustained. Many times I feel God's healing presence when I hear Bill pray for my needs or fears. Often he is able to put into words the thoughts that I haven't yet been able to express. I often do the same for him.

Be careful not to preach in prayer. We have talked to several couples who are resistant to praying together because they feel as if the spouse uses prayer to bring up the flaws or weaknesses of the other. One husband said, "My wife can bring up old arguments and drive home her point in prayer. I feel violated and taken advantage of when she does that." Be careful that neither of you uses prayer as a weapon against your spouse. Nothing will kill prayer time together more quickly than if your spouse feels on trial or intimidated or attacked by your prayers. Prayer with your spouse is not a time to unload all the gripes you have toward each other.

It is grace that redeems, that saves. It is grace that restores and facilitates love. Prayer can bring grace into our marriages. Marriage—more than any other relationship—offers a forum for honest definition of oneself to one another. We believe it is of utmost importance for those of us who follow Christ to invite His presence into our marriages through prayer.

HOW TO USE THIS BOOK

We designed this book to be a keepsake prayer journal that will help you grow in your prayer life and in your marriage relationship, allowing God's presence to touch various aspects of your life. The book can be used on a variety of levels: as a journal, as a record of God's faithfulness, as a springboard for your own prayers together, as an inspiration for your personal growth, as a guide for learning how to pray. Make the book work for you. Allow it to open up your prayer life and enrich your marriage.

You will find fifty-two chapters in this book—one for every week in the year, if you choose to use it that way. Each chapter focuses on one specific element or attribute (such as "Intimacy," "Anger," "Handling Money," "Honesty," "Tenderness") that

will form the basis for praying for your marriage.

The chapters are grouped together by sections so that each section conveys a specific theme. In this way, each section of five or six chapters is like a concentrated course on a particular theme for your marriage.

The list of fifty-two characteristics is not an exhaustive one. It does, however, represent the concerns couples voiced in our marriage surveys. Certainly you should add additional things to your prayer agenda as they become apparent to you. In many ways, this book is like a template to help you start or be more focused in your prayers as a couple.

The book is designed so that you can use it individually or together. If you have a spouse who is reluctant to read the book with you at all, the book will still provide a valuable tool for you personally to invite God's presence into your marriage. It will also work very well if you decide to go through the book as a couple. All of the features of the book will work well either way.

We hope this book becomes a useful tool that you use virtually every day or at least every week. The Scriptures, prayers, insights, and quotations provide a springboard for the discussion questions, and the journal space is for your personal notes/reflections/prayers/goals.

Our prayer for you is that this book will help you grow closer to each other and to God. It will also indirectly help you resolve conflict because God is the great healer, including the healing of our relationships. We know from experience that prayer will give your marriage a new boost and provide both of you with some spiritual insights about yourself as well as your marriage.

If your spouse is reluctant to begin this process, it is fine to start by sharing needs or prayer ideas and then praying separately for these. Another good way to begin is to take the topics of this book and simply agree on which topic will be the prayer topic for that week. Each of you can pray alone if that feels more comfortable and then share with each other what the Lord impresses on you.

To help you better understand the function of this book and each element of the chapters, we'll walk you through a typical chapter.

Prayer
The opening prayer helps you start thinking about the specific attribute covered in that chapter. This prayer can be used as a springboard for you to begin your own prayers. We believe that prayer is conversation with God. In that conversation we can say anything we feel about the attribute. We can confess our fears and frustrations. We can acknowledge our own weaknesses. We can let God know we don't know how to approach the subject. And we

can include specific things we know about our marriage regarding this particular attribute.

You may begin by using this prayer as your prayer if it feels comfortable, or you can use it as a thought process to spark your own prayer. Remember, *you* are praying for the presence of God in your marriage in this specific area.

Scripture

We included Scripture passages that give some insight about the specific attribute. Again, use these verses as sparks to ignite your own interest in what Scripture teaches about the attribute. You may want to do your own word- search study to find significant passages. These verses are for your meditation. In Psalm 1 David tells us that it is delightful to meditate on the Word of the Lord. To meditate means to contemplate, to ponder, to reflect, or to "chew on." As you chew on these Scripture passages, the Lord will bring new insight to you. Throughout the day as you do a chore, drive to work, or wait for the copy machine to warm up, engage your mind in a meditative moment on the Scripture verses chosen for each attribute.

Insight

We have attempted to make the attribute more real by sharing illustrations and reflections from our own marriage as well as from others who have shared insights with us. We hope that these thoughts and stories will inspire you with insight, conviction, and added knowledge. You may find the insights useful if you discuss the attribute with your spouse.

Reflection

Because we have always learned from what other people say about a subject, we have included quotations from other sources. Some quotations are from classic works of men and women who pondered these thoughts many years ago, and some are from our contemporaries who live at a hectic pace in our culture.

Let's Talk about It

The questions in this section are designed to stimulate your own thinking and elicit discussion with your spouse. You may think of other more appropriate questions that fit your marriage. The idea here is communication that will give both of you some insight. If you think that discussing the issues could provoke conflict, you could agree to some ground rules for these discussions. One might be that you agree not to use accusing tones or to speak in diminishing ways. Another might be to find a new approach to discuss the issue if it is something you have had arguments about before and have not been able to resolve. Another idea is to agree to discuss the issues with a trustworthy couple who may also be using this book. It may be less threatening to do this in the context of a group at first. Just remember, the idea is to communicate, and this means listening as well as speaking.

Your Notes / Reflections / Prayers / Goals

This final section in each chapter allows you to record your insights, reflections, decisions,

prayers, and goals. We have tried to keep this open so that it fits however you may choose to use this book. Here are several suggestions that may help you decide how to use this space.

If you are going through the book alone, you can use this space as a place to journal your thoughts, prayers, hurts, and hopes. It then becomes a private journal for you to reflect on this attribute of your marriage. You can also write some of your prayers to the Lord here and later check these to see how God has answered them. It is also a great place to jot down other Scripture passages the Lord has revealed to you about the attribute addressed in the chapter.

If you are going through the book as a couple, you can use this space to record your insights, covenants, and goals as a couple. After discussing and praying about the attribute, commit to some specific things you will do. If you write them down, you can then go back and measure the progress you are making in that area. If you find that you need more space to write, use a notebook that will become a companion to the book. Some couples told us they will use the space to expand on prayers and Scriptures that mean something to each of them. Others indicated they will buy a second book so that each spouse will have a journal record of the couple's growth.

A third idea for this section is to use it as a place to write a note to each other. This will work especially well if you have agreed to start this process by praying separately for the same attribute during a given week. You can then go to the book and write a note of affirmation, apology, or resolution to your spouse.

By using this section in one or more of these ways, it will make your "Keepsake Pages" in the back of this book even more meaningful over the years because you will have good notes to review as you write in your annual Keepsake Pages. (Keepsake Pages are explained in more detail below.)

Even if you are using the Notes space to write goals and prayers, it is a good idea to write notes to each other from time to time. Use stationery or cards to write each other love notes, notes of affirmation, notes of apology, etc. Any form of communication that is healing, reconciling, affirming, or hopeful will help your marriage.

When you see significant growth in a particular area in your marriage, make sure to do two things: Thank God for His work in your marriage, and affirm your spouse about the growth you see.

Keepsake Pages

In the back of this book you will find what we call "Keepsake Pages" that are designed to help you reflect and chart progress in your marriage on an annual basis—maybe on an anniversary or on the first day of the year. You will notice some specific questions that act as a template for your reflections. We have included space there for five years of reflection. Whether you use them for five subsequent years or you use them less often, it will one day give you a more complete and long-term picture of how God worked in your marriage.

Some couples told us that they plan to go through the entire book year after year. They said that the topics and attributes covered in this book are ones they know they will need to review regularly.

Someday, you might even consider giving this prayer journal to a child or grandchild as a keepsake inheritance gift at their own wedding, to prove to them that God does indeed help us make life together more fulfilling and meaningful.

PRAYING FOR THE PRESENCE OF GOD IN OUR RELATIONSHIP

Friendship

Consideration

Communication

Listening

Giving the Best Gifts

Little Things

Seeking Mentors

PART 1

PRAYING FOR THE PRESENCE OF GOD IN OUR

FRIENDSHIP

1

A friend loves at all times.

Proverbs 17:17, NKJV

PRAYER

Lord, I thank You for my best friend—the one You have given me to walk with through life. Thank You for showing me by the life You lived what real friendship is. I pray that we will never take each other for granted and that I will remember to give my spouse my best and to protect our friendship always. Amen.

SCRIPTURE

"Two people can accomplish more than twice as much as one; they get a better return for their labor. If one person falls, the other can reach out and help. But people who are alone when they fall are in real trouble" (Eccles. 4:9-10).

When our sons were growing up and beginning the dating process, I (Bill) would sometimes ask them about the girls they would mention in their conversation. Often our sons would reply, "She is just a good friend, Dad." I remarked to them that a good friendship is a strong basis for a good marriage. Invariably they would roll their eyes at me since marriage was the last thing on their minds at the time.

But I wanted to give them a message: Friendship is a powerful basis for a good marriage. In fact, I think friendship is more lasting than physical and sexual attraction. Physical attraction is a very powerful force and is a necessary element in choosing our spouse, but it can tend to dominate our decision-making process. Good marriages need more than physical attraction, and one of the most important elements is friendship.

Friendship has an enduring quality about it. It is the solid foundation that will make a marriage thrive and last through the years. Friendship in marriage is the commitment to walk together. As the little saying goes, "Today I married my best friend."

The qualities that initially attracted Nancie and me to each other were our common interests. In fact, the first time we met, we were on a double date—but with other people. I spent most of my time talking with Nancie, almost to the point of neglecting my date! I think that Nancie's date was a little upset with me for distracting her from him, too. But Nancie and I just hit it off. We were both interested in ministry, music, speaking, ideas, and books. We enjoyed the outdoors and realized that family was important to both of us. Thirty years later, the friendship that began that night is more important to us now than ever.

What are the marks of a true friendship?

Friendship offers acceptance. Friendship in marriage allows you to be *you*. It gives you a place where you don't have to prove yourself and you don't have to change one another. You and your spouse may be very different from each other, but your friendship will allow you to recognize and accept those differences.

Friendship is based on honesty and respect. Let's face it, it can be difficult to be in a close relationship for many years and yet live peacefully and joyfully. As friends in a marriage, you must learn how to tell each other the truth in love and to respect yourself and your spouse. Proverbs 27:6 reminds us, "Faithful are the wounds of a friend" (NKJV).

Friendship offers understanding. It's undeniably true: men and women are very different from one another. Often we think differently, see the world differently, and come to marriage with different expectations and beliefs. Your friendship with your spouse means that you both will make a commitment to understand the other's point of view.

Friendship shares a mutual focus. Friendships deteriorate when people focus only on personal needs—what *I* need, what *I* want. Many romantic relationships begin that way, but it's important to move past that to a more reciprocal, balanced relationship. Mature friendship involves "looking out" at the world together so that you can share a focus on a work project or your family or your ministry involvements.

Friendship gives time and energy. Friendship in marriage takes initiative. You can't take your dearest friend on earth for granted and have the friendship thrive. The relationship needs protecting. It needs the investment of time and care. It needs to be protected from the crush of the pressures of life. Guard yourself from seeing your spouse as a commodity, someone you need, someone who provides a service like cleaning the house or mowing the lawn. Choose always to see your spouse as that unique person you married—your best friend. Protect your friendship by proactively scheduling time together to remember the joy and fun there is in being best friends.

As Nancie and I look back over the years, we see that while there are many needs that we can meet in one another—sexual, romantic, emotional—the role of friendship has been a strong part of the foundation in our relationship. As we have talked to other couples about their marriages, we are seeing how underrated and yet how very important friendship within marriage is.

Lord, teach us what it means to truly love and accept one another. When the days get busy and we are tempted to take one another for granted, remind us that we are best friends. Help us to give one another our best, not the leftovers of the week. May our friendship honor You and be a reflection of the kind of friend You are to us. In Jesus' name, amen.

Friendship

REFLECTION

"In survey after survey, at least 80 percent of couples in successful long-term relationships report that they have become best friends. . . . They feel accepted with their faults and have come to accept their mates as a package deal."

Dr. Georgia Witkin, "How to Keep Intimacy Alive"

"Love does not consist in gazing at each other but in looking together in the same direction."

Antoine de Saint-Exupéry, quoted in *Quiet Moments for Couples*

LET'S TALK ABOUT IT

1 What qualities first attracted you to each other?

2 In what three ways can you strengthen your friendship with your spouse?

YOUR NOTES/REFLECTIONS/PRAYERS/GOALS

_____

_____

_____

_____

_____

_____

_____

_____

_____

_____

_____

_____

_____

_____

Friendship

CONSIDERATION

2

Don't be selfish; don't live to make a good impression on others. Be humble,

thinking of others as better than yourself. Don't think only about your own affairs,

but be interested in others, too, and what they are doing.

Philippians 2:3-4

PRAYER

Lord, I confess my indulgent, selfish ways. It seems that my human nature just naturally demands to think of me first—my wants, my needs, my agenda. Give me renewed grace to consider my spouse first. Teach me what it means to lay down my life, as You laid down Your life for me. Help me to see that true happiness comes from giving, not taking. Amen.

SCRIPTURE

"Love does not parade itself, is not puffed up; does not behave rudely, does not seek its own"
(1 Cor. 13:4-5, NKJV).

Consideration is the acting out of love. It is the *doing* of love. When we are being considerate, we think about what our spouse needs. We ask, What can I do to make my spouse's life better? Then we go the extra mile to do it.

Betsy, a friend of ours, had very difficult pregnancies with both of her sons and had to stay in bed for months at a time. Because she is a very active person, this was hard for her. She was so grateful that her husband considered her needs and acted to meet them. "Marty was amazing. If no one else was coming over that day to help me, he would pack a lunch and put it by the bed. He came up with some fabulous dinners, too. And he never acted as if those gestures were an imposition."

Marty was paying attention to what was going on in Betsy's life, and he tried to make things better for her. In being considerate, he gave his wife a feeling of safety and refuge.

Being considerate is a practical way to show love, honor, and respect. Here are some other ways in which we show consideration to our spouse. We can

- take seriously our spouse's ideas and dreams;
- understand our spouse's need for space or for being together;

Consideration

- be fair about sharing responsibilities and tasks;
- be sensitive to the occasional "bad day" and show our spouse that we care in small but significant ways.

Making life easier for our spouse may involve making ourselves easier to live with. Sometimes I need to stop and look at my relationship with Bill through *his* eyes and ask hard questions: "Do I make Bill's life more difficult, or do I ease his load? What is it like for Bill to be married to me?" Then I need to make an honest assessment of where I can be more considerate of him.

Not long ago Bill talked with me about a frustration he was experiencing. I listened briefly, then offered advice. I was surprised when he perceived my comments as criticism. I just thought I was being helpful. But when I thought about his reaction, I realized that I hadn't really stopped to consider his feelings. He had been feeling hurt by the situation he was telling me about. And rather than sense his hurt, I had given him advice.

When we show consideration by taking into account our spouse's feelings, we strengthen our friendship and build respect and love. Consideration says, "I am aware of you. I am aware of your fears, your insecurities, your physical needs. I am aware of your time commitments, your pressures, and your limitations."

Consideration does not take the other person for granted. Consideration stops to ask a spouse, "How do you feel about this?" before taking on a commitment, especially if the commitment will have an impact on the spouse.

Years ago we saw this kind of consideration demonstrated by Harry Downey, an older man with whom Bill worked on a church staff. As a young husband, Bill watched as Harry defined consideration by how he treated his wife, Nan. When people would call and invite Harry to attend meetings or other functions, he would say, "Well now, I would like that very much. But let me check with Nan first to be sure she hasn't already planned something."

Harry considered Nan's needs in other ways. When he had a day off, he would take her out to lunch. And not just anywhere. Bill heard him asking around to find the nicest restaurants in the most beautiful settings, even if they were a hundred miles away.

Nan blossomed as a result of Harry's consideration—common courtesy, as it has been called. He treated her like a queen, and she felt like one. It always impressed me to see Harry—a towering man at six feet four inches—opening the car door or holding a chair for his diminutive wife, who was almost a foot and a half shorter than he was. Some people would say those were only little things. But Nan didn't think they were so little. Through her husband's considerate gestures, she heard him say, "You are so special. You are worth every consideration to me!"

Lord Jesus, how considerate You were of people when you lived on earth! You fed them when they were hungry; you healed them when they were sick. You washed your friends' feet for them and took time for people many others didn't consider worthwhile. Lord, we ask Your presence to invade this area of our lives. By Your example and Your presence, make us aware of how we can offer healing and comfort to one another simply by being more considerate. Amen.

REFLECTION

"All the beautiful sentiments in the world weigh less than a single lovely action."
James Russell Lowell, quoted in *Quiet Moments for Couples*

"If I am inconsiderate about the comfort of others, or their feelings, or even their little weaknesses; if I am careless about their little hurts and miss opportunities to smooth their way . . . then I know nothing of Calvary love."
Amy Carmichael, *IF*

LET'S TALK ABOUT IT

1 In what specific ways have you done or said something considerate to your spouse in the past week?

2 Ask your spouse how you can be more considerate of him or her in the coming week. If you discuss this chapter with your spouse, also share one specific way in which he or she can show consideration to you.

YOUR NOTES/REFLECTIONS/PRAYERS/GOALS

_____

_____

_____

_____

_____

_____

_____

_____

_____

_____

_____

_____

_____

Consideration

COMMUNICATION

3

Death and life are in the power of the tongue.

Proverbs 18:21, NKJV

PRAYER

Lord, You have said in Your Word that there is tremendous power in words. So often, Jesus, I have heard my own mouth say things that I instantly wished I could recall. But the words are gone from me like arrows that penetrate my spouse's heart. Help me to remember to think before I speak, to give words that heal, not destroy. Help me to speak words of encouragement, affirmation, and hope to my spouse. In Your name, amen.

SCRIPTURE

"The tongue is a small thing, but what enormous damage it can do. . . . It is full of wickedness that can ruin your whole life. . . . Blessing and cursing come pouring out of the same mouth. Surely, my brothers and sisters, this is not right!" (James 3:5-10).

What penetrating, true words these are from the New Testament book of James. Words can have a powerful creative effect on us. They can bring inspiration, or they can bring doubt. They can bring hope, or they can bring fear. They can bring comfort, or they can bring great emotional pain. And the closer our relationship, the more impact our words have on each other. As kids, we learned the phrase "Sticks and stones may break my bones, but words can never hurt me!" It's not true in a marriage, and it may not be true in other places. Words *can* hurt us. They can also heal us.

Can you remember words that went like arrows into your soul, cutting you down and making you feel worthless? Often words like "You never [name the gripe]" or "You always [name the bad habit]" jump from our lips without our thinking how condemning or hurtful they may sound.

Similarly, can you remember words that fell like raindrops on your soul, nurturing you and making you feel valuable? Affirming, helpful words can motivate us and shape our lives in positive ways.

In marriage—this closest and most challenging of relationships—we have the opportunity either to build each other up or to tear each other down with the words that we speak. And by the words that we use, we can advance the presence of God in our relation-

ship or hinder it. With our words, James says, we can offer blessings or curses.

Where do our words come from, and why do hurtful words bubble to the surface? Jesus said our words come from our innermost beings, our hearts (Matt. 15:18-20). And, as we know, our hearts are often full of destructive thoughts and feelings.

In our culture we have somehow come to believe that if we feel something, we are obligated to speak it. This is not a godly philosophy. Not all things that we *feel* should be said. What our parents told us is true: It's important to think before we speak. We need to consider if saying what we feel will build up or tear down our spouse. Will it heal or hurt? Will it strengthen our relationship or weaken it?

Sometimes it is best to be quiet (especially if we are very angry) so that we can speak the truth in love. Not that we stifle the truth; it is never loving to withhold the truth. But we must learn to convey truth in ways that confront the issue without attacking the person.

Certain words should never be said. Words that diminish each other and words that threaten the relationship should be banished from our marriage vocabulary. Tom and Susan told us, "When we got married we made a covenant with each other to never even jokingly refer to divorce. The word is just not in our vocabulary."

What incredible power you have in your marriage by the words that you speak. You can validate your spouse by affirming him or her by your words. You can also enhance your entire marriage relationship by thinking about the positive things about your spouse and by speaking those things instead of the negative.

Words of encouragement are powerful. Gina related to us, "After a difficult year with the sudden death of a parent, a complicated estate settlement, and purchasing a business, my husband and I were both on overload. One day in tears I asked him, 'Will we ever get through this?' He looked at me, incredulous, and said, 'Oh, of course we will, honey! We're in this together.' Somehow his simple response was a defining moment in our marriage." Words of encouragement help us to go on, even in the most dreary times.

We all need encouragement, and we all need forgiveness and restoration when we've spo-ken harsh words. One Sunday morning Bill and I sat in church together, and remnants of leftover angry words from an argument the night before made me feel defeated. The congregation sang, "Think about His love; think about His goodness. Think about His grace that's brought us through."

Bill reached over and took my hand and squeezed it, and I squeezed back, reminded of the powerful effect our words can have. I remember praying that morning for God's presence to saturate our hearts with His grace so that from those grace-filled hearts could flow words that heal.

Thank You, Lord, for reminding us of the immense power that we have in one another's lives through the words that we say. First of all, Lord, change our hearts. Be Lord of all of us—our hearts, our thoughts, our intents—so that what comes out of us will be a blessing. Teach us what it means to bring life—and not death—to each other through the words we say. In Jesus' name, amen.

Communication

REFLECTION

"Marriage is a long conversation, chequered by disputes."
Robert Louis Stevenson, quoted in *Speaking of Marriage*

"Words have great power. With a word God called into being the beauty of the cosmos. With a word he can silence the most threatening forces of evil. His word brings life. As he speaks and acts in the world of sin, he pushes back the chaos by his powerful word. God also calls husbands and wives to use our words to push back the chaos and shape our lives into order and beauty. He calls us to use our words to bring life to those who hear them."

Dan B. Allender and Tremper Longman III, *Intimate Allies*

LET'S TALK ABOUT IT

1 What words or statements tend to shut down communication in your marriage?

2 What words or statements help advance God's presence in your marriage?

YOUR NOTES/REFLECTIONS/PRAYERS/GOALS

_____

_____

_____

_____

_____

_____

_____

_____

_____

_____

Communication

PRAYING FOR THE PRESENCE OF GOD IN OUR

LISTENING

4

My dear brothers and sisters, be quick to listen, slow to speak,

and slow to get angry.

James 1:19

PRAYER

Forgive us, Lord, for so often listening to one another only with the intent to reply. Help us to learn to truly listen to one another with our hearts as well as our ears. Teach us to give each other undivided attention at least once every day. May we seek not just to be understood but also to understand. Amen.

SCRIPTURE

"The hearing ear and the seeing eye, the Lord has made them both" (Prov. 20:12, NKJV).

I hope the listening problems in your marriage are not as serious as this couple's were. According to a newspaper story, a man driving in South Carolina was surprised when police officers stopped his van and asked him if he was missing something. The man looked puzzled, not knowing what the officers were talking about. Finally one of the officers asked the man where his wife was. Turning to the passenger side of the car, the man was shocked to find that his wife wasn't there. It turns out he had left her in a parking lot when they had stopped at a rest area at two o'clock in the morning. Apparently the man had gone to the bathroom, had gotten back into the car, and had driven away—without his wife! "I've been talking to her the whole time and wondered why she didn't answer," the confused man told the officers. I guess this man was used to the silent treatment.

I wonder if some couples go through an entire life together without really hearing one another. How often we see couples in restaurants sitting together, not talking. Not that a comfortable silence isn't good now and then, but it is often easier to listen to strangers because we have no expectations of them— they have no hooks in us. With a spouse, the dimension changes. Sometimes it can be very hard to listen because we feel we must solve the problem or because we are hearing the same thing over and over again.

Yet how healing it is simply to be heard. Our friend Marylou told us about a significant moment early in her marriage. She had had an extremely devastating day at work and had come home in tears. She tried to tell her husband what had happened, but she was too distraught to talk very well. Her husband, a fix-it type of guy, simply held her in his arms. He listened, saying little. She says, "He didn't offer any solutions. He just offered his precious arms, where I felt safe. He let me sob and blurt out my feelings. I didn't need his words that day. I just needed him to hold me and listen."

Someone once said, "Being heard and feeling loved are so similar that the two are nearly indistinguishable." Marylou agrees. "My husband's gestures that day communicated to me his understanding and love."

True listening means using more than just our ears; it means using our hearts. Hearing the words and listening with my heart are two totally different things. One is a biological mechanism; the other is a godly gift. I find it much easier to "hear" my spouse's words than to "listen" to my spouse's heart.

True listening involves asking, "How are you?" and really wanting to know. It involves watching body language and other unspoken expressions. In marriage, as in other relationships, our words tend to sail past each other, through each other, or over each other. And if the words do land, we tend to bounce them back in the form of opinions and agendas as if we're playing a sort of verbal Ping-pong.

What are some of the obstacles to listening?

- Not giving eye contact. (Like reading the paper or watching TV while our spouse is trying to have a conversation.)
- Mentally preparing our response while the person is speaking, rather than concentrating on what the person is saying.
- Body language that says things like "I'm bored" or "I've heard enough" or "That's ridiculous!"
- Frequent interruptions to make our point known.
- Giving simplistic advice before we've heard the whole story.
- Acting as if a person's feelings are not legitimate, telling the person, in essence, to "buck up and get over it."

In order to listen effectively, we need to be quiet. That means not only that we need to refrain from speaking but also that we need a quiet inner spirit, opening the heart like a soft basket trying to catch what the speaker is trying to say.

The deepest part of our self is made alive and whole when we are heard. We feel "visible." Heartfelt listening means caring about what is important to the person speaking, putting yourself in that person's shoes. To communicate well, to have an intimate conversation, to be honest from the bottom of our souls, we must listen without judgment.

Great listeners do not react; they simply keep loving and hearing with their whole heart. Great listeners have a sense of inner stability. I believe we learn to be great listeners by learning to be still and hear God's voice to us through His Word and through quiet time with Him. When we practice cultivating this awareness of listening and when we bring the awareness of His presence into our marriage, it is a powerful dynamic.

Lord, You are truly the Great Listener because You see past the surface deep into our hearts. First of all, help us to listen to Your still small voice, to be aware of Your abiding presence. And then, Lord, give us the courage to listen to one another, welcoming Your presence in our every conversation. Amen.

REFLECTION

"Listen to all the conversations of our world, between nations as well as those between couples. They are for the most part dialogues of the deaf."

Paul Tournier, *To Understand Each Other*

"Every effective communicator must learn the skill of 'active-listening.' It's called 'active' because the listener has a responsibility. He works at grasping what the speaker is saying and attempts to help him express those feelings. This is extremely difficult to do, especially when we hear criticism or something we disagree with. Our inclination is to tune out or correct what is said. . . . But when we do active-listen, we convey a clear message of acceptance. Whether or not we agree with what is being said, we convey the message that this person is worth being heard."

André Bustanoby, *Just Talk to Me*

LET'S TALK ABOUT IT

1 Recall a time when you felt your spouse really listened to you. What were the circumstances surrounding the experience, and why do you remember it?

2 Ask your spouse, "How am I at listening to you? How can I improve?"

YOUR NOTES/REFLECTIONS/PRAYERS/GOALS

_____

_____

_____

_____

_____

_____

_____

_____

_____

_____

GIVING
THE BEST GIFTS

5

If you give, you will receive. Your gift will return to you in full measure,

pressed down, shaken together to make room for more, and running over.

Whatever measure you use in giving—large or small—it will

be used to measure what is given back to you.

Luke 6:38

PRAYER

Lord, You have given us many gifts—our lives, the very air we breathe, the water we drink, the food that nourishes us, the beauty that daily surrounds us. Knowing we are made in Your image, we too have gifts that we can give one another as symbols of our love. Teach us how to give good gifts—genuine gifts—to one another. Amen.

"Giving a gift works wonders" (Prov. 18:16).

As marriage partners, we are in a unique position to give our spouse gifts that no one else can give him or her. These gifts are often intangible but important to mental and emotional health. Here are some wonderful things you may not have considered on your gift list for your spouse, but I assure you they are some of the best gifts you could possibly give.

Affirmation. We all need to feel validated and affirmed. Remind your spouse of his or her good qualities, God-given talents, and potential, especially when your spouse is emotionally down or going through tough times of doubt. You, more than anyone else, have the power to build up your spouse in times like these.

Attention. Sometimes our undivided attention toward our spouse can be a wonderful gift in communicating that we are listening and that we understand. Our attention can give our spouse tremendous strength to carry on. A wife who has been with toddlers all day needs to know that her husband cares about her day and wants both to listen to her concerns and to share his. A husband who has been involved in conflict in an office all day needs to know that his wife will set aside some time

when the two of them can take a walk and talk about his stresses.

Hope. Bring hope to your spouse by reminding him or her that life is essentially good. Speak optimistically whenever you can. Follow the apostle Paul's instructions to think—and speak—about things that are true, noble, right, pure, lovely, and admirable.

Thoughtfulness. Create "sunshine" for your spouse by surprising him or her with thoughtful gestures. A note tucked into a suitcase for a husband away on a trip or a bouquet of flowers for a wife who is under pressure not only is a romantic gesture but also brings the sunshine of hope into what otherwise might be a dreary day. A husband who comes home from work and tells his wife he is ready to roll up his sleeves and take over the task of feeding and bathing the kids while she gets some needed time to herself is giving the wonderful gift of thoughtfulness. A friend said about her husband, "Mike just isn't sentimental, but he gives me Mike-gifts. He may forget Valentine's Day, but he never forgets to fill my car with gas and keep the oil changed!" Nancie's mother used to love a Mounds candy bar now and then, but, living on a farm far from town, she didn't have ready access to stores. Nancie remembers times her father came home late from a school-board meeting and with his shy schoolboy grin handed her mother a Mounds candy bar.

Occasional extravagance. Once in a while, it is both exciting and fun to be extravagant. I love surprising my wife with occasional out-landishness. For instance, one Christmas when I was a pastor, Nancie was pregnant again and sick. Although finances were very tight, I decided to sell a little red pickup I owned in order to have money for a much-needed vacation. I surprised Nancie with tickets to Hawaii. (Plus, I got to go to Hawaii too!) For Nancie's fiftieth birthday, I organized a train trip, with twenty-five of our friends, to a Montana lodge where Nancie had fond childhood memories. She had no clue about the trip until we arrived at Union Station in Portland and everyone yelled, "Surprise!"

Togetherness. Another wonderful gift we can give each other is the gift of our presence.

Recently, I wanted Nancie to go with me on a business trip so we could be together. Although I think she really wanted to stay home, she sensed my desire to be together and readily agreed to go. The trip turned out to be a wonderful memory for both of us, and I am so grateful that she took the time to go with me. I travel a lot, and having Nancie with me occasionally is a marvelous gift!

There are many other intangible gifts we can give. The above list is just a sample. Ask, "What is in my power to give that I alone can give?" You are in that intimate place to delight and please your spouse with a gift that says, "Here is a token of my loving care for you."

Lord, thank you for giving us the gift of a spouse. What an incredible privilege it is to receive this gift. Help us learn how to give gifts that build up our spouse, gifts that reflect our hearts. May our giving be thoughtful, creative, and wise. May we not get caught up in the world's way of giving, but may we learn to give as honest demonstrations of our love. Amen.

REFLECTION

"Total commitment is the willingness to share everything—especially ourselves. Each of us is to give all of ourselves to all of our spouse. Life is no longer a solo journey, but a joint endeavor. Two giving themselves freely and equally of everything they can, fulfills the spirit of total commitment."

Steve Stephens, *Experience the Best*

"A man stops off at a florist and brings his wife a single rose in the evening, a girl makes her lover a lemon pie with just the tartness he likes, a wife makes arrangements for her husband to take the caribou-hunting trip he thought he would never afford—these are not the goo of sweet emotion, they are the stuff that comes from resolution and determination, and they are strong mortar."

Alan Loy McGinnis, *The Romance Factor*

LET'S TALK ABOUT IT

1 What gift, more than anything else, do you need from your spouse? What gift does your spouse need from you?

2 Think of an act of thoughtfulness you can give your spouse this week.

YOUR NOTES/REFLECTIONS/PRAYERS/GOALS

Giving the Best Gifts

_____

_____

_____

_____

_____

_____

_____

_____

_____

_____

PRAYING FOR THE PRESENCE OF GOD IN OUR

LITTLE THINGS

6 . . . .

Catch us the foxes, the little foxes that spoil the vines,

for our vines have tender grapes.

Song of Solomon 2:15, NKJV

PRAYER

Lord, how easy it is for me to fall into destructive patterns of behavior . . . wasting time, consuming things I should not, falling into destructive patterns of communication that hurt rather than heal. These habits affect my marriage. Help me, Lord, to see the destructive habits that I have and to break away from them. Give us wisdom to help each other in these "little things" without complaining or nagging. Amen.

SCRIPTURE

"We who are strong ought to bear with the failings of the weak, and not to please ourselves" (Rom. 15:1, RSV).

I'm convinced that marriage is mostly made up of "little things." What were the little things that first attracted Bill and me to each other? I loved his take-charge attitude, his attention to detail. He tells me he was drawn to my gentle, laid-back approach. What are the little things that can drive us crazy thirty years later? His need to be in control can be most irritating; my lack of confrontation frustrates Bill. In other words—the same little things!

It's true that our greatest strength tends to become our greatest weakness, and so it is with the little things in our lives. A little irritation can become the small rock in the shoe, the speck in the eye, the burr under the saddle.

We must be careful not to ignore the little things in our marriages. Our habits and manners may seem insignificant to us, but they can become major irritants to our spouse. Our personal hygiene habits, even though they are personal, affect our spouse. How we use our time can frustrate our spouse. We can easily write off our own personality quirks by saying, "Oh, that's just me," but those quirks can be upsetting to our spouse.

Not much has changed through the centuries in the challenge of putting up with each other's uniqueness. In his book *Husbands and Wives,* William Petersen tells the story of Martin Luther's marriage to Katie. At the time of the marriage, the former priest was forty-one; the former nun was twenty-six.

Luther wrote, "There is a lot to get used to in the first year of marriage. One wakes up in the morning and finds a pair of pigtails on the pillow that were not there before. . . . Before I married, no one had made up my bed for a whole year. The straw was rotting from my sweat. I wore myself out with work during the day, so that I fell into bed oblivious of everything." That all changed when Katie came into the picture and took charge of his household. They were both strong, verbal people with many differences, yet their marriage became a strong one. Luther taught that marriage must be worked on and prayed over. "To get a wife is easy enough, but to love her with constancy is difficult . . . for the mere union of the flesh is not sufficient; there must be congeniality of tastes and character, and that congeniality does not come overnight. . . . Love begins when we wish to serve others."

Luther's comment gives us direction about how we are to respond to the quirks and irritants we see in our spouse: "Love begins when we wish to serve others." How can we serve our spouse and bear with his or her flaws?

First, we must take care not to become so obsessed and focused on our spouse's flaws that our focus creates resentment and bitterness. If it does, our response can become worse than the actual flaw, and we can become part of the problem. This may be one reason Jesus taught about removing the log from our own eye before we try to remove the speck from someone else's (Matt. 7:3).

Second, how can we bear with each other's faults in a Christlike way?

Ask the Holy Spirit's help to love with patience and kindness. God loves us in spite of our flaws and sins. We need His help to love our spouse in spite of his or her irritating quirks and faults. We cannot do it on our own.

Remember that we have our faults too. Some days I am so grateful that Bill's love for me extends beyond my weaknesses. When I am aware of how much he puts up with to live with me, I grow in my ability and willingness to live with the little things that irritate me about him.

Speak the truth in love. We must be willing to talk with our spouse about the habits that frustrate us. How we do this is very important, making sure that our motive is to help the relationship, not hurt the spouse.

Let it go. After you have said what you must, let it go. Focus on your spouse's positive qualities. Enjoy daily life together. Don't let the little things become mountains that are obstacles to your growth as a couple.

Lord, help us to see how we can change the little things that irritate our spouse, and help us to bear with our spouse's flaws and quirks. May we be sensitive to one another's perspective on the habits we've grown so used to and have the courage to change if they are damaging our marriage. May we have understanding to know when we need to back off and not try to change one another. Help us know the difference between a bad habit that needs to be changed and a personality trait. In Jesus' name, amen.

REFLECTION

"Good habits are not made on birthdays, nor Christian character at the new year. The workshop of character is everyday life. The uneventful and commonplace hour is where the battle is lost or won."

Maltbie D. Babcock, *Treasure of Inspiration*

"There are as many miracles to be seen through a microscope as through a telescope. Start with little things seen through the magnifying glass of wonder, and just as a magnifying glass can focus the sunlight into a burning beam that can set a leaf aflame, so can your focused wonder set you ablaze with insight. Find the light in each other and just fan it."

Alice O. Howell, *The Dove in the Stone*

1 In an atmosphere of mutual love and respect, agree to share with one another two things about your spouse that annoy, embarrass, or irritate you. Are you willing to initiate change in yourself first?

2 Tell each other why changing that particular habit would be beneficial to your marriage.

YOUR NOTES/REFLECTIONS/PRAYERS/GOALS

_____

_____

_____

_____

_____

_____

_____

_____

_____

_____

_____

_____

_____

_____

Little Things

PRAYING FOR THE PRESENCE OF GOD IN OUR

SEEKING MENTORS

Follow my example, as I follow the example of Christ.

1 Corinthians 11:1, CEV

PRAYER

Thank You, Jesus, for the inspiring example of certain couples that are in our lives. It is gratifying to see Your grace at work within these marriages of our friends whom we admire and wish to emulate. May we always keep our eyes on You, knowing the reason these couples inspire us is because they are following You. And help us to have the kind of marriage that others can follow, too. In Christ's name, amen.

SCRIPTURE

"Set an example for other followers by what you say and do, as well as by your love, faith, and purity" *(1 Tim. 4:12, CEV).*

We recently did a survey asking couples how they felt about marriage mentors. All of them said they wanted to *have* a mentoring couple, a couple whose example they could follow. Yet none of the couples wanted to volunteer to *be* a mentoring couple. This seems to suggest that most people do not consider their marriage worthy of emulation. Most of us are so aware of our failings and imperfections that we conclude we are not capable of becoming mentors for others. Let's look at both finding mentors and becoming mentors.

What are marriage mentors? On one hand, marriage mentors are people who will let you look at their marriage close-up, will let you ask them questions about their relationship, and will share with you what they have learned about making a marriage work. These mentors are often conscious that you have chosen them to be models you would like to follow. On the other hand, marriage mentors can simply be people after whom you want to pattern your marriage. You may not even know these people well. You may see them only from a distance, maybe through the books they have written or through things you have heard about them. These people are not consciously aware that you see them as models, but you are influenced by them nonetheless.

What do you look for in marriage mentors? Look for couples whose lives you admire and who are strong in the areas in which you want to grow. If teamwork is important to you, find couples who model effective teamwork in household management or ministry. If mutual respect is important to you, identify couples who affirm each other's differences and encourage growth in each other. If having a vibrant friendship with your spouse is important to you, look for couples who enjoy each other's company. If spiritual maturity is important to you, seek out couples who work effectively to grow together spiritually.

Look for couples who have gone through some of the same life passages you are experiencing. If you are students, look for couples who have gone through school while they were married. If you move a lot, try to find couples who have thrived through transitions from one place to another. If you are in ministry, identify couples who have successfully faced some of the stresses unique to ministry couples. If one of you travels a lot, spend time with other couples who have built strong marriages even though they were apart from each other frequently.

Over the years, Bill and I have been privileged to be exposed to some great couples, and their examples have taught us much. We have three other couples with whom we meet once a year for a retreat, and we pray for each other throughout the year, holding one another accountable to follow Christ and to honor Him in our marriages. Although we know each other well and are honest about our weaknesses, we have learned something from each couple. As we've thought about the couples whom we see as mentors, we've noticed that they have certain qualities in common:

1. They are committed to each other. Their marriage is a vital part of their lives, not merely an incidental relationship. They do all they can to protect it.

2. They want to place God first in their lives. Their relationship to Him is their main focus—not their work or their social life or recreation, even though those may be important.

3. They actively show the fruit of the Spirit toward each other. Bill and I call them "Galatians 5 couples." They display love, joy, peace, patience, kindness, goodness, faithfulness, gentleness, and self-control toward each other. Even in their humanity, even with their own quirks—and we all have them—they are willing to grow in their relationship to one another in these specific ways.

4. They are human enough to be "fun." They know that life is too important to take too seriously. They know how to laugh at themselves and have a good time.

How do you find mentor couples? First of all, we've found we have to look for them. Mentoring is usually not a scheduled relationship. It is more likely to be informal and spontaneous. Small groups or marriage retreats can facilitate getting to know these couples better.

How can you be marriage mentors to others? As you mature in your marriage, pray that God will help you to give from what you have. Be willing to allow several couples to see your marriage more closely. Mentoring others can be an exciting growth opportunity. As is true with any kind of modeling experience, when we are aware that other people are watching us, we often take more seriously our responsibility to reflect God's character.

Lord, how well we know our own imperfections. And yet Your faithfulness does a deep and lasting work in us. Thank You for bringing into our lives couples who have encouraged us in our marriage and who reflect who you are. May we freely invest in the lives of others what You have taught us through our friends. Amen.

REFLECTION

"Empowering has to do with the investments people make in one another. It is what happens when we concern ourselves with the question, Is the person with whom we are friend, spouse, or family a growing person because he or she is in intimate connection with us?"

Gail and Gordon MacDonald, *Till the Heart Be Touched*

"Truth must be made flesh through loving relationships. People today hunger for intimacy and a sense of being connected to other persons. . . . Nuclear families have often exploded into pieces, neighbors come and go every few years, and friends who know one's entire personal history are rare. . . . When truth is practiced in love, the result is unity.

Bill Hybels, *Tender Love*

L E T ' S   T A L K   A B O U T   I T

1 What qualities would you look for in a mentoring couple? What couples do you know with these qualities? How can you build relationships with these couples?

2 Are you ready to be a mentor couple? If not, what can you do to better prepare your marriage to be a better example? If you are ready, how are you making yourself available to other couples who could use your example?

YOUR NOTES/REFLECTIONS/PRAYERS/GOALS

_____

_____

_____

_____

_____

_____

_____

_____

_____

_____

Seeking Mentors

PRAYING FOR THE PRESENCE OF GOD IN OUR PHYSICAL LIFE

Fitness

Affection

Lovemaking

Recreation

PART 2

PRAYING FOR THE PRESENCE OF GOD IN OUR

FITNESS

8

Do you not know that your body is the temple of the Holy Spirit who is in you,

whom you have from God, and you are not your own?

1 Corinthians 6:19, NKJV

PRAYER

Help us, Lord, to master the personal discipline in our physical habits to be good stewards of the bodies You have given us. May we remember that we are Your temples. Help us to make wise choices in what we put into our bodies and how we stay physically fit. Help us to realize that doing this is an act of love toward each other so that we can give our very best to our marriage. Amen.

SCRIPTURE

"I keep my body under control and make it my slave, so I won't lose out after telling the good news to others" (1 Cor. 9:27, CEV).

We often take our healthy bodies for granted until something goes wrong, and then we realize how our health has an enormous impact not only on our own life but also on our spouse's life. While we cannot predict major illnesses and physical limitations that happen, we can use preventive measures to take care of ourselves through a good diet and consistent exercise.

Several years ago I (Nancie) went through some major health struggles and lived with a diagnosis of systemic lupus erythmetosis, a chronic illness, for four years. Bill was patient and considerate, but the chronic pain and fatigue was hard on our relationship. After I had a complete workup at Mayo Clinic, it was determined that I did not have lupus after all. My physician believed that the way I was handling stress in my life was the major cause of my problems. I realized I was getting a wake-up call and determined to go home and do what I could to be a better steward of my body. Since that time, I have learned valuable lessons about the importance of exercise, enough rest, proper diet, and a more balanced life. Consistent walking is something I know I must do—it is not an option. I still struggle with overcommitment, but I've learned to take time to relax because if I don't, I am not able to give our marriage what it needs.

Bill has contended with a weight problem most of his adult life, but he keeps trying and is experiencing some success. We both know

our vulnerabilities and challenges. I need to present to Bill a more relaxed and available wife; Bill needs to keep pressing toward the goal of weight loss.

Despite our individual struggles, we know we cannot wait for perfect, physically fit bodies to have a great marriage. We are not the Hollywood ideal! The important principle is realizing that taking care of our bodies in a balanced way is an act of love for each other and that we will do the best we can, making allowances for each other's humanity. We don't have to be Olympic athletes. We can start quite simply where we are, getting more exercise and making good lifestyle choices. Being physically fit does help our physical relationship. It's fun to be able to bike, hike, golf, or do work projects around the house together.

In her book *Pillow Talk,* Karen Scalf Linamen wrote, "I used to think that diet and exercise were about weight and looks. Now I know better. The primary benefits are *not* reduced weight and a streamlined shape, although those can certainly be by-products of a consistent regimen. . . . Now I know that the primary benefits of healthful living—benefits that can be recognized almost immediately—are *energy* and *confidence.*"

There is no getting around it—the health of one spouse does affect the other. Good nutrition and exercise should be a lifestyle, not just something we work at now and then. Living in a committed, long-term marriage is a marathon, not a sprint. As the years pile on, Bill and I are seeing how precious health is and how essential it is to do all we can to be good stewards of our physical selves.

Sometimes illnesses happen, adding pressure to the marriage. Chronic, long-term illnesses are particularly difficult. But here is also an opportunity to exercise true patience, love, and consideration. We need the actual physical affirmation and acceptance of each other, imperfections and all. In the book *The Marriage Collection*, Shirley Cook suggests, "Don't be self-conscious about the shape of your body. Maybe you think it is too fat or too thin, but it is yours—and your mate's. You belong to each other. Just keep your body clean, dress it neatly, and then, as the occasion arises, give your mate *all of you.* Love

him for himself. Love that person who lives inside the body. Love covers a multitude of sins—along with the lumps and bumps of an imperfect shape."

In our body-conscious society, it's important to look at the whole picture of physical fitness and remember that our bodies are given to us by God to honor Him and to serve and love one another. We can encourage each other to take loving and respectful care of ourselves.

Lord, it's tempting to get caught up in the world's way of fitness, and fitness can seem a difficult goal to achieve. And yet we realize that You have made us. We are Yours, and You have made us for each other. May we honor each other, and may we honor and discipline our bodies, knowing that they house Your Spirit. May our stewardship of our physical bodies increase our effectiveness as a couple to serve Your kingdom. Amen.

REFLECTION

"From our survey, by far the greatest fears that spouses have for the future were related to health concerns—either for themselves or their spouse. Of those in the survey ages fifty and over, 59 percent said that the thing they feared most was death and/or illness, compared with only 19.5 percent of those under fifty. . . . Investments in your health are investments in your friendship with your spouse. . . . How long has it been since you've had a physical? When have you taken a hard look at your diet? Are you getting the exercise you need? If you want to enjoy the second half of life, take our advice: Take care of yourself; if you don't, no one else will!"

Dave and Claudia Arp, *The Second Half of Marriage*

"One of the commitments we have, besides telling the truth and truly being oneself, is to take care of ourselves separately. Somebody told me that a long time ago, and I had no idea what they were talking about. If you truly love someone, the highest gift you can give them is to take care of yourself."

Janmarie Silvera, quoted in *The Heart of Marriage*

L E T ' S   T A L K   A B O U T   I T

1 What areas of physical health/fitness do you struggle with? What can you do to improve your health and fitness?

2 How are you handling your spouse's physical "flaws"? How can you use this as an opportunity to demonstrate God's grace?

YOUR NOTES/REFLECTIONS/PRAYERS/GOALS

_____

_____

_____

_____

_____

_____

_____

_____

_____

_____

PRAYING FOR THE PRESENCE OF GOD IN OUR

AFFECTION

9

Let the husband render to his wife the affection due her,

and likewise also the wife to her husband.

1 Corinthians 7:3, NKJV

PRAYER

Oh, God, how I sometimes need to be held! How I need to be hugged and touched in tender ways that are so vital to my emotional health. Help me to learn to give and receive affection. I know that through affirming touch I can give my spouse healing, assurance, and restoration. And, Lord, thank You for holding me, too! Amen.

SCRIPTURE

"Love each other with genuine affection, and take delight in honoring each other" (Rom. 12:10).

How healing it is to affirm one another with a tender touch of kindness and with physical affection. Some of us did not learn within our families of origin how to be affectionate, and we have to work harder at it than those who grew up in a home where hugs, loving words, and caresses were part of the daily communication.

Also, life can be hectic, and affection can get lost in daily demands and expectations. Little irritations can pile up into big resentments, and we may not feel like being affectionate. But when we lose the sense of affection, we lose the sense of being loved. It's ironic that *acting* affectionate—even if we don't *feel* it—can restore feelings of love.

Dr. Harville Hendrix, a marriage therapist, has seen many couples locked in power struggles, and these couples couldn't seem to get past their conflicts to a place of affection. Although insight into their childhood wounds was helpful for these couples, it wasn't enough to make them act lovingly toward each other once again. In his book *Getting the Love You Want,* Dr. Hendrix relates that he was surprised to learn that when he was able to get the spouses to treat each other the way they did in happier times, they began to feel more affectionate toward one another. Hendrix writes, "Almost without exception, when couples began artificially to increase the number of times a day that they acted lovingly toward each other, they

began to feel safer and more loving. This intensified the emotional bond between them, and as a result they made more rapid progress."

This principle seems to have a biblical precedent. In the book of Revelation, the message to the church in Ephesus included these words: "I have this complaint against you. You don't love me or each other as you did at first! Look how far you have fallen from your first love! Turn back to me again and work as you did at first" (Rev. 2:4–5). While these words were spoken to a church that had lost its devotion to Christ, the principle is a good one for us as married couples: Work at it as you did at first.

Remember how you and your spouse acted when you first fell in love? Do those things again. Treat each other the way you did when you first were in love, and watch the results.

Affection is not to be confused with the act of sex. Affection has more to do with attitudes and acts of caring for each other. Affection involves having fond and tender feelings and actions toward another person. It is a special form of connection with each other.

Touch can be a powerful healer that couples can offer to each other. Hugs, running your fingers through each other's hair, a gentle back massage, or a squeeze of your spouse's hand at the right moment tells your spouse that you are there and that you care. Sometimes our spouse just needs to be held for a while. Just holding someone can breathe new energy and hope into one's spirit. An arm around your spouse's waist while taking a leisurely walk pours love and affection into the other without a single word needing to be spoken.

Brenda, married five years and with two small children, told us, "My husband and I got so busy raising kids, working, and taking care of our house that we literally forgot to connect in every way—physically, emotionally, and spiritually. It's amazing what happened when my husband and I went away together for a few days recently and were absolutely lost in each other again. It's wonderful!"

But it's possible to "connect" in the ordinary days, too. My mother used to tell me after the too-early death of my father, "Don't wait for some day to enjoy each other. Learn to savor every day." If you wait to feel affectionate toward one another, you may wait a long time. Use your imagination, your creativity. You can offer affection to your spouse in many ways: through embracing, holding hands, tender looks, admiration, and compliments.

It's important to find out what affectionate gestures and words are meaningful to your spouse. You don't want to spend time giving your spouse a back rub, assuming that it is a meaningful gesture of affection, only to learn that your spouse finds it irritating or painful. Take the guesswork out of affection by talking about it with your spouse. Find out what makes your spouse feel loved, and tell your spouse what makes you feel loved.

Tell your spouse what affectionate gestures are meaningful to you. If you like it when your husband puts his arm around you in public, thank him when he does it the next time. If you feel loved when your wife scratches your back when you watch television together, tell her that you appreciate it.

Lord, how soothing is a gentle touch, especially in this violent and anger-filled world. May we take time to give each other the affection we both crave. May we put aside our pride and self-reliance to tell one another of our need for affection. May we bless one another with loving glances and tender touches, demonstrating our love. In Jesus' name, amen.

Affection

REFLECTION

"In our marriage, Chris and I often have said as we crawled into bed at night, 'This is the best time of day.' Why? God knew when He ordained marriage that touching would produce the comfort, assurance, and drawing emotionally from each other so needed by weary mates at the end of a long day."

Evelyn Christenson, *What Happens When We Pray for Our Families*

"Little expressions of affection and approval mean more to a woman than a man imagines. She wants to be remembered, adored, cherished, complimented, listened to; she wants to have her feelings validated even when they seem childish or unreasonable to her husband. She needs to be made to feel feminine by being protected, cared for, looked after, to have affection often without sex, to be accepted especially when she feels unacceptable to herself."

Cecil Osborne, from *The Marriage Collection*

LET'S TALK ABOUT IT

1 On separate sheets of paper, complete the following sentence in as many ways as possible: "I feel loved and cared for when you . . ."

2 Think about a caring and loving behavior that you have always wanted but never asked for, and complete this sentence: "I would like you to . . ."

YOUR NOTES/REFLECTIONS/PRAYERS/GOALS

_____

_____

_____

_____

_____

_____

_____

_____

_____

_____

Affection

PRAYING FOR THE PRESENCE OF GOD IN OUR

LOVEMAKING

10 . . . .

My beloved spoke, and said to me: "Rise up, my love, my fair one, and

come away. . . . O my dove, in the clefts of the rock, in the secret places

of the cliff, let me see your face, let me hear your voice;

for your voice is sweet, and your face is lovely."

Song of Solomon 2:10-14, NKJV

PRAYER

Lord, You created us as sexual beings, and You have given us to one another to provide joy and fulfillment in this physical part of our relationship. We ask that You give us understanding to make this a mutually satisfying relationship. May we guard our thought life and focus our sexual desires on each other. Help us to respect and fulfill the needs and desires of our spouse so that we may keep the passion between us for all our years together. Amen.

"The wife's body does not belong to her alone but also to her husband. In the same way, the husband's body does not belong to him alone but also to his wife. Do not deprive each other except by mutual consent and for a time, so that you may devote yourselves to prayer" (1 Cor. 7:4-5, NIV).

I N S I G H T

Some of us may feel uncomfortable about inviting God's presence into our sex life. We think, *God, in our sex life?* But after all, God is the Creator of the wonderful gift of sex. He has given us sex not only to bring children into our lives but also to nourish and protect the mystery of our becoming one flesh with our spouse.

Some years ago we published a *Virtue* magazine interview with Cliff and Joyce Penner, highly respected marriage therapy experts. In the interview the Penners talked about the value of a healthy sex life within marriage. In response to the article, we received a letter from an older, never-married reader who was tired of reading articles about sex. She wrote, "I have no use for sex! It's better to abolish it!" Bill posted the letter on his bulletin board just to get a smile out of me. Sex is an integral part of our God-given selves and is a powerful bond that holds an intimate marriage together. Here are some suggestions that can help your lovemaking:

Talk to each other about your sexual wants and needs. In their article the Penners said, "If this is an area of difficulty for you—talking to each other about your sex life—we recommend a couple get a book and read it together. We don't recommend professional help first. The couple needs to start talking to each other, and a good way to start is to use a book. Discussion will happen much more spontaneously if they're reading to each other than if they read the book separately and then try to discuss it. If a couple then finds that they do in fact need professional help, they will have defined their problem much more clearly through dialogue. Self-help is quite beneficial because (1) the majority of people will not seek professional help, (2) many are in places where there isn't a trained professional, and (3) many people will not go for counseling because of their inhibitions or financial limitations."

Take personal responsibility for your sexual wants and needs. The Penners went on to say, "One of the reasons that there is a lot of sexual dissatisfaction among women is that they don't take responsibility for themselves. Many women think that their husbands should instinctively know where they like to be touched, what will work and what won't. People think you can learn how to relate sexually in three easy steps and that everyone is the same. It just isn't that way. People change from moment to moment, and needs vary from one person to another. The only way to be really satisfied is if a woman takes the responsibility to communicate to her husband and actively pursue that satisfaction."

Never force your spouse to perform sexual acts that he or she does not enjoy. Sex in marriage must be mutually satisfying. There are many ways to fulfill your sexual desires with each other without having to force your spouse to perform sexual acts that he or she feels are unpleasant, wrong, or distasteful. And all couples should avoid the use of pornography or sexual fantasies that involve other people.

Let go of resentment and unforgiveness. This may be easier said than done; but it's also true that if we wait until conditions are perfect to have a good sex life, it may never happen. I (Nancie) used to believe that *after* we got all our differences settled, *after* we communicated effectively, *after* Bill gave me roses and was

sweet all week, then we would have a terrific love life. When we withhold sex because of our feelings, we are giving a conditional love, a please-me-or-pay attitude. Sometimes it's best just to open my arms and heart and set about enjoying my husband, and talk later. The problems that seem insurmountable before lovemaking take on a completely different perspective later.

Let lovemaking be the special gift that God intended it to be. The beautiful, erotic Song of Solomon describes the loved one calling to his lover, "Come away, my beloved." The gift of lovemaking that we can offer one another invites us to "come away" from life—away from the pressures, the agonies of daily responsibilities.

Lord, we thank You for creating us the way You have. Thank You for the strong bond of our physical love that strengthens our one-flesh. We pray that You will be present in every aspect of our lives. May we use the gift of our lovemaking to do just that—to increase and enhance our deep love and fidelity to one another. Amen.

Lovemaking

REFLECTION

"*We feasted on love, every mode of it, solemn and merry, romantic and realistic, sometimes as dramatic as a thunderstorm, sometimes comfortable and unemphatic as putting on your soft slippers. She was my pupil and my teacher, my subject and my sovereign, my trusty comrade, friend, shipmate, fellow-soldier.*"

C. S. Lewis, quoted in *Getting Ready for a Great Marriage*

"Sexual intercourse involves the opening up of ourselves to our partner. The nakedness alone is symbolic that nothing is hidden and that one is at a point of extreme personal vulnerability. For sexual intercourse to be most meaningful, it requires the unhindered sharing of our innermost thoughts, feelings, and very being. This surrender of our private identity to another is both frightening and satisfying, for in the sexual relationship we willingly expose ourselves to the risk of rejection.

Steve Stephens, *Experience the Best*

LET'S TALK ABOUT IT

1 What are the most common complaints you have about your sex life? Have you discussed these, in detail, with your spouse?

2 Discuss with each other what steps you can take to enhance your sex life. Plan a lovemaking weekend together soon!

YOUR NOTES/REFLECTIONS/PRAYERS/GOALS

_____

_____

_____

_____

_____

_____

_____

_____

_____

_____

RECREATION

11

Enjoy life with your wife, whom you love, all the days . . .

that God has given you.

Ecclesiastes 9:9, NIV

PRAYER

Thank You, Lord, for giving us the opportunity to enjoy life and health. We want to be companions, best friends who enjoy many of the same things. Help us to develop mutual pursuits in relaxing and recreating together. Truly, all good things come from You. Teach us what it means to play together, to celebrate the joy of the present moment. Amen.

SCRIPTURE

"A merry heart does good, like medicine, but a broken spirit dries the bones" (Prov. 17:22, NKJV).

Lois Jean Davitz surveyed four hundred divorced men between the ages of twenty and forty-five and revealed some surprising contradictions to popular myths about why marriages fail. "What virtually every man in our study cited as decisive to the failure of the relationship was the lack of companionship," she said in her book *Living in Sync: Men and Women in Love.*

And how did these men define companionship? Doing enjoyable things together with their spouse, spending recreational time together. But these men also defined what companionship was *not*. It was not merely doing parallel activities such as sitting together and watching television. It was not going on outings with their children. It was not sex, although a desire for sex may grow out of companionship.

Recreation

Davitz saw a man's desire for female companionship as a shift in expectations. "In the past," she said, "men often turned to other men for companionship, but today, they'd rather spend time with their wives." Unfortunately, this shift comes at a time when many women are feeling overwhelmed by their multiple roles as wage earners, home managers, wives, and mothers. Wrote Davitz, "As women struggle to meet expanded challenges, there's a very real danger that the men they love are being squeezed out of their lives."

As busy couples, it's easy for us to neglect our need for recreation. But we all need time to have fun together, to get away from our normal routines for activities that allow us to rebuild and restore our balance.

Sometimes we have to search for common ground to find a recreational activity we both enjoy. Bill and I parent together, work together, sometimes speak together, and write books together. Because most of what we do together is on the serious side, we found that we were really missing having fun together. Bill loves to golf, so I thought I would take it up. After a few disastrous games, I decided I agreed with the person who described golf as a "good walk spoiled."

Gina was more successful when she took a risk and plunged into one of her husband's recreational activities. "I'd heard that to keep my marriage alive, I needed to be involved in my husband's 'fun' things. So I took up scuba-diving lessons with my husband. When it was time for our certifying dive in thirty-six-degree water, I was terrified. My husband wanted me to do this with him so badly he tried everything to coax me into the water. He told me, 'I know you feel that your life is in jeopardy, but trust me. I won't let anything happen to you. I'll be beside you every minute.' I took the plunge, and now I'm an avid diver too!"

Bill and I didn't let my golf disaster keep us from having fun together, however. We bike together and explore local history. We've also realized that we can leave room for *his* fun (golf doesn't seem fun to me) and *my* fun (there's nothing I like better than to hike in the mountains for a few miles), but we need to keep finding common ground for us to share recreation as a couple.

One special area of recreation that Bill and I share is boating. When we get on our boat in the summer, we are in a completely different world. We love being outdoors, and something about being on the boat makes us feel like kids again. Several times we have been tempted to sell the boat because it seems extravagant to use it only for such a short season, and yet it has brought us such enjoyment and restoration that we have decided we will probably always be boaters, even if we have to rent one.

Years ago we had friends who worked hard at their ministry together. But they had no life outside of their work. They were always tense, and their tension grew into animosity toward each other. We found it difficult to be with them. As years went by, their children seemed to want nothing to do with God or the church. While it's impossible to judge a marriage from the outside, I wonder if this couple's situation would have been different if they had spent more time in recreational activities together.

What are you modeling to your children? When they see you, do they see two best friends enjoying each other? Remember that life is brief, and we only have this moment to savor each other. Don't be so consumed by work—even worthwhile things—that you forget to enjoy time with your spouse. It may take some coaxing to convince your spouse to "come out and play," but enjoying recreation together is the very essence of a sense of playfulness that makes life worth living.

Lord, You have created us to enjoy one another. Help us to find recreation that restores and refreshes us. Awaken us to the joy in the world all around us. May we be relaxed and spontaneous enough to celebrate life together. May we take risks to enter one another's world and be life companions in the fullest sense possible. Amen.

Recreation

REFLECTION

"It is possible for 'in love' newlyweds to quickly develop two different worlds like separate continents without bridges unless they make a concerted and consistent effort to spend their free time together, developing absorbing interests in common, and doing the tasks of life in partnership, side by side."

Ed Wheat, *Love Life for Every Married Couple*

"Being playful is the cotton candy of any meat-and-potatoes relationship. It's the . . . let's-have-a-party, let's-skip-work-and-go-to-the-beach, let's-rent-three-videos-and-watch-them-all-tonight state of mind that lifts a relationship from the tedious and banal to the extraordinary and effervescent. We forget to play, or we never learned how. We are worked so hard and so long by life as it is—and by our own ambitions—that most of us don't play nearly enough."

Daphne Rose Kingma, *Garland of Love*

LET'S TALK ABOUT IT

1 What activities do you both enjoy? How are you incorporating those things into your relationship and leisure time together?

2 What are your areas of friction about recreational activities or time? How can you make compromises and find mutual ground?

YOUR NOTES/REFLECTIONS/PRAYERS/GOALS

_____

_____

_____

_____

_____

_____

_____

_____

_____

_____

Recreation

PRAYING FOR THE PRESENCE OF GOD IN OUR EMOTIONS

PART *3*

Intimacy

Anxiety

Anger

Passion

Purity

Emotional Differences

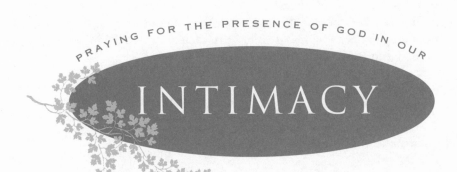

PRAYING FOR THE PRESENCE OF GOD IN OUR

INTIMACY

12

For this reason a man shall leave his father and his mother and cling to his wife and they shall become one flesh. Both the man and his wife were naked and they felt no shame in each other's presence.

Genesis 2:24-25, MLB

PRAYER

Lord, show us what it means to have true intimacy with each other. Help us to be so open with one another that we can talk together about anything. Teach us what it means to create a safety zone that will allow us to be truly "one flesh" in its most intimate sense. Lord, thank You for showing us that the closer we come to You, the closer we will be to one another. Amen.

SCRIPTURE

"You are like a private garden, my treasure, my bride! You are like a spring that no one else can drink from, a fountain of my own" (Song 4:12).

When Bill and I were first married, he gave me a beautiful pendant that has two leaves with a pearl in the middle. To me, the pearl between those two gold leaves symbolizes intimacy. I see in this gold pendant the God-shaped vacuum that only He can fill. The two leaves surrounding the pearl represent the holy ground between Bill and me. In his book *Seeds of Contemplation,* Henri Nouwen wrote, "Can real intimacy be reached without a deep respect for that holy place within and between us, that space that should remain untouched by human hands?"

While intimacy in marriage includes sex, true intimacy is much more. It is a closeness that results from sharing our deepest selves, our entire being. In many ways this kind of intimacy is a spiritual discipline. We can cultivate intimacy in the following ways:

Respect each other's uniqueness. Intimacy asks us to respect each other. Bill and I have learned painful lessons about mutual respect. We have discovered that each of us is created in different and unique ways. *Different* does not mean "wrong" or "imperfect"; it simply means different. Each of us brings something unique and precious to our marriage relationship, and if we do not respect our spouse's uniqueness, we tend to desecrate our potential for intimacy.

Think of it this way. In order to play musical harmony, it takes two parts. If you are both singing the same note, you may have unison, but you do not have harmony. Harmony is much sweeter music and more interesting than a one-note monotone. The same is true in marriage. The harmony of two people blending their differences is far more beautiful and pleasant than the sound of two people insisting that they must be alike in everything.

For years, Bill and I both tried to change each other in certain ways. (He wanted me to "get more organized." I wanted him to "be more spontaneous and less planned.") We have now learned that our differences can be objects of appreciation and value rather than objects of irritation. We each bring strength to the relationship in our own special way. Our differences round us out and bring balance to our lives.

Give your relationship some "white space." While working with magazine design for many years, Bill and I learned an important concept: The "white space" on a page is just as important as the copy or art. A cluttered page with no white space does not invite the reader into the subject. The same is true for a marriage. When a marriage relationship is cluttered with activities and agendas, it leaves little time for two married people to explore the deepest parts of their relationship. The relationship has no space to breathe. In discussing intimacy, Henri Nouwen also said in *Seeds of Contemplation,* "Can human intimacy really be fulfilling when every space within and between us is being filled up?"

Intimacy demands white space. Sometimes, all that spouses need is time to be together without feeling obligated to speak. Intimacy is a language all its own, and words are not always necessary to express its virtue. Much can be accomplished when couples hold hands while taking a walk or spend time hugging or holding each other.

Allow each other a safe place to be vulnerable. It is nearly impossible for a marriage to be truly intimate if we do not feel comfortable being vulnerable with our spouse. Being vulnerable in a marriage is risky when one or both people are unsure if vulnerability will be met with unconditional protection and acceptance. All of us need someone to whom we can confess all our fears, divulge all our secrets, express our outlandish thoughts, and show our deepest emotions. We do this best with the most intimate of our circle, namely our spouse. When we ridicule our spouse for his or her emotions or when we betray each other's confidence by talking about it with others, we diminish the potential for intimacy by making our spouse feel it is risky to be vulnerable.

Intimacy is holy ground. When your spouse lets you inside the deepest places of the heart, be careful to tread softly and recognize that you are in a sacred place. Take care to nurture the intimacy you have with your spouse. When the demands of life press in on you, the intimacy you have built will protect you, comfort you, and refresh you.

Lord Jesus, help us not only to seek intimacy but also to become people with whom true intimacy is possible. Teach us to respect this sacred ground, to be willing to risk vulnerability, and to give unconditional permission to our spouse to be intimate with us in every way possible. Amen.

Intimacy

REFLECTION

"If two people who have been strangers, as all of us are, suddenly let the wall between them break down and feel close, feel one, this moment of oneness is one of the most exhilarating, most exciting, experiences in life."

Erich Fromm, *The Art of Loving*

"Table and bed are the two places of intimacy where love can manifest itself in weakness. In love men and women take off all forms of power, embracing each other in total disarmament. The nakedness of their body is only a symbol of total vulnerability and availability."

Henri Nouwen, *Seeds of Contemplation*

1 In what ways does your marriage relationship demonstrate intimacy? How can you deepen your intimacy?

2 Are you comfortable being vulnerable with your spouse? If not, discuss this with your spouse and find ways to lessen the hindrances to vulnerability.

YOUR NOTES/REFLECTIONS/PRAYERS/GOALS

_____

_____

_____

_____

_____

_____

_____

_____

_____

_____

_____

_____

_____

_____

Intimacy

PRAYING FOR THE PRESENCE OF GOD IN OUR

ANXIETY

13

Don't worry about anything; instead, pray about everything. Tell God what you

need, and thank him for all he has done. If you do this, you will experience God's

peace, which is far more wonderful than the human mind can understand.

Philippians 4:6-7

PRAYER

Lord, it is not Your will that we be consumed by anxiety. As we come together to pray, teach us to trust You with our lives. We also pray that in doing so, we will learn to know the presence of Your peace. Help us not to approach You with an attitude of fear but with the confidence of faith. Amen.

SCRIPTURE

"Anxiety in the heart of man causes depression, but a good word makes it glad" (Prov. 12:25, NKJV).

In a magazine survey Nancie and I conducted a few years ago, we discovered that men and women tend to suffer anxiety over different things. Men worry about finances and issues of control, while women worry about safety and issues surrounding relationships.

A young man said to me recently, "My wife seems to worry about everything. Every time I come home late, she thinks that either I've had an accident or that I'm having an affair. Now that we have a baby, she's afraid that something awful might to happen to our child. She won't leave him with a baby-sitter, even for a couple of hours. I'm getting weary of all her worry! It seems to be consuming our entire relationship."

God does not want us to live with constant fear, worry, and insecurity. Those emotions create distress for any marriage, robbing us of joy. How can you move from a spirit of anxiety to a spirit of faith within your marriage?

Recognize God as the source of your security. When anxiety descends on you, remember that God is your rock, a strong foundation in times of stress. God is your hiding place. He is the loving Father who provides for you. He has numbered the very hairs of your head.

Put your trust in God. Sometimes it is not enough to merely recognize that God is our source. We must actively choose to trust Him. One of our problems today is that we have so many resources of our own that we

are reluctant to trust God with our needs. When we insist on our own control, we are saying to God that we do not trust Him with our lives. This attitude brings part of the anxiety we may feel because we have taken a responsibility that really belongs to God alone. When anxiety overwhelms us, we can take comfort in God's promises to us: "Don't be afraid, for I am with you. Do not be dismayed, for I am your God. I will strengthen you. I will help you. I will uphold you with my victorious right hand" (Isa. 41:10).

Help each other overcome fear and doubt. Unbelief can creep into our minds in very subtle ways. As a spouse, you are in the best position to recognize when your husband or wife needs to be helped out of a funk. It is tempting at times to blame God for the bad things that happen. Some of us fall prey to a theology that teaches that God is busy running around the planet arranging cancers and automobile accidents. As I heard one pastor put it, "Some people think that God is a vengeful God, and the only reason He tolerates us is because Jesus tells Him He has to." However, God's nature is one of love, grace, and redemption. When you are going through trials and problems, remind each other that God promises to be with us in our adverse situations.

Look around. You can always find someone who is worse off than you. Sometimes we get so caught up in *our* problems, *our* misfortunes, our worries, that we fail to see others around us who face much more severe or difficult problems than we do. Recently Nancie and I became "stressed" over the loss of her bracelet, which was not only expensive but of sentimental value because I had given it to her as a surprise for our thirtieth wedding anniversary. In the busyness of an active day with many other people in many places, we did not know if it had been stolen or if it had simply slipped off her wrist. At the moment we were fretting over this loss, news flashed across our television screen about several children who had been shot and two who had been killed by a very disturbed boy in a school located just two hours from our home. Our "problem" was not even in the same stratosphere as the problem these parents and students were having to deal with. We immediately forgot about our "loss" and began to pray for the lives of those involved in this tragic shooting. (And then, the next day we got a call that the bracelet had been found!)

Exercise a spirit of thankfulness. God teaches us in His Word that having a thankful heart is the key to overcoming anxiety. Thankfulness releases our spirit to trust God with our circumstances. It causes us to see things from a new faith-filled perspective. It brings joy and hope into our hearts. Paul said, "Think about things that are pure and lovely and admirable. Think about things that are excellent and worthy of praise" (Phil. 4:8).

Lord, we acknowledge You as a good and gracious God, and we want to rely on You for our needs. Help us to trust You with our lives and our circumstances. Help us to exercise a spirit of thankfulness, and in doing so, to banish anxious thoughts. In Jesus' name, amen.

REFLECTION

"Our emotions are the movements of our soul. They are the sensations we experience that bear the labels of joy, grief, pain, disillusionment, love, delight, warmth, astonishment, fright. They are the stirrings of our inner persons reflected in our cellular shells. Also, emotions are the subterranean shifts in feeling we encounter that aren't necessarily activated by sight, hearing, taste, or smell—though they may be. These inside movements, stirrings, or sensations may change several times an hour. They may occur in multiples, forming duets and trios that sometimes produce harmony and at other times create dissonance."

Ed and Candee Neuenschwander, *Two Friends in Love*

"Life is war, and marriage provides us with a close and intimate ally with whom we may wage this war."

Dan B. Allender and Tremper Longman III, *Intimate Allies*

LET'S TALK ABOUT IT

1 What things cause you anxiety? How can you and your spouse trust God with these concerns?

2 As an antidote to anxiety, make a list of the things for which you are thankful in your marriage.

YOUR NOTES/REFLECTIONS/PRAYERS/GOALS

① FOR OUR FRIENDSHIP (GROWING)

② LAUGHTER

③ BEING ABLE TO DISCUSS THINGS WITHOUT ALWAYS ARGUING

④ WORKING TOGETHER

⑤ HONESTY (ABLE TO BE OURSELVES)

⑥

PRAYING FOR THE PRESENCE OF GOD IN OUR

ANGER

14

Those who control their anger have great understanding; those with a hasty

temper will make mistakes.

Proverbs 14:29

PRAYER

Lord, how often we struggle with this very human emotion of anger. Usually our anger is not righteous anger, but anger brought about by our own selfishness. Lord, help us to learn to use our emotions in a constructive way. You, Lord, have created us with emotions—but teach us how to harness our feelings in ways that build, not destroy. In Christ's name, amen.

SCRIPTURE

"What is causing the quarrels and fights among you? Isn't it the whole army of evil desires at war within you?" (James 4:1).

Anger

"Shelley, look at this Visa bill!" screamed her husband, Dave. "I can't believe you'd be stupid enough to buy another dress when you know how tight our budget is!" Dave slammed his fist into the kitchen cupboard next to Shelley's head and stomped out of the room. Dave's anger goes much deeper than the Visa bill, but neither he nor Shelley is aware of that. All Shelley knows is that Dave's frequent eruptions frighten her and leave no opportunity for calm communication. She wonders if someday he will erupt and physically harm her. She wonders if she should leave.

Conflict in marriage is inevitable. Sometimes conflict produces feelings of anger. Anger in itself is not bad. Anger becomes destructive, however, when we do not handle it well.

Some people, like Dave, lose their temper when they are angry. In the process they hurt their spouse with their explosive words and behavior. Other people tend to suppress their anger. When we suppress anger, it often explodes later, when the pressure reaches the boiling point. Our suppression of anger can be just as damaging to ourselves and our relationships as our outbursts of anger.

So, if it is not appropriate to lose our temper and if it is harmful to bury our feelings, what is an appropriate way to express our anger? Here are some thoughts to consider:

Practice responding to a situation rather than reacting to it. To *react* is to have a knee-jerk out-burst. In the heat of anger, we often try to take immediate action in a situation. We speak and act without thinking. However, unless it's a case of extreme emergency, reacting in such a way is a bad response. When we react without thinking, we often feel remorse for our harsh words and actions. Once words are spoken or physical action taken, it is hard to reverse the damage. Even if we say that we are sorry, our spouse will still feel the sting of our words or the pain of our actions.

To *respond* means to be more thoughtful before we speak or take action. When we respond, we take a time-out and consider why we are angry. I have discovered that if I discipline myself to pray about whatever it is that has triggered my anger, I often gain new control and insight regarding the situation.

Guard your words. Words are powerful. When someone to whom we have pledged our love says hurtful things out of anger, it is hard not to be angry in return. Again, we must respond rather than react. If you need to confront your spouse with an issue, be sure that you attack the issue and not your spouse. *Never* threaten your spouse with words of divorce, abandonment, or physical violence; these expressions are always inappropriate.

Learn to recognize the emotions behind the anger. Anger is usually the result of hurt, frustration, or fear. If we learn to recognize when we are hurt, we can express that hurt appropriately before it turns into anger. Saying "I felt hurt when you laughed at my idea about our vacation" is better than saying in anger, "OK, then, plan the stupid vacation yourself." If Dave had been able to recognize and express his frustration—and even fear—that Shelley was overcharging their credit card, he may have been able to express his emotion before it turned into rage. He and Shelley may have been able to talk about their problem if he had said, "Shelley, I've just looked at our Visa bill, and I am frustrated that you charged a dress. If we can't keep our charges in line, we are going to be in big trouble."

Focus your anger where it belongs. Proper expression of anger is usually centered on sin, evil, and injustice. Unless your spouse has betrayed you in some specific way, the anger you feel is probably an immature emotion about an irritation or about not getting your own way. When two married people stand together and focus their anger on the threats to their marriage or family, they become allies rather than enemies.

In their book *The Angry Man,* David Stoop and Stephen Arterburn offer some good suggestions for wives of angry men. However, the advice is appropriate for both men and women. Be a friend, not a parent. Appreciate rather than nag. Affirm, don't criticize. Give your spouse space instead of crowding him or her. Give, don't withhold. Hold your spouse responsible so you won't be codependent.

Lord, help us not to use our anger destructively. Help us to think before we speak. Help us to understand our spouse so well that we can sense when other factors may bring stress to our relationship. Help us to express our hurt, frustration, and fear in constructive ways. Finally, help us to be quick to affirm our spouse and give the best we have. Amen.

REFLECTION

"When we pray for each other, the attitude of our own heart becomes softer and more forgiving toward our mate. It is impossible to earnestly pray for someone and be filled with hatred for them at the same time. If we will start to pray, even if angry, the Lord will give us peace. As you pray for your partner, you will find yourself letting go of your animosities, your reservations, your pettiness, and your insistence upon having your own way."

Patrick Morley, *Two-Part Harmony*

"Conflict is an integral part of all close friendships and of every good marriage. Intimacy breeds conflict. You can't have one without the other. In fact the closer the two people become, the more they experience the oneness that was God's intention for married people, the more they open themselves to friction."

Joyce Huggett, *Creative Conflict*

L E T ' S   T A L K   A B O U T   I T

1 When you become angry, are you more often hurt, frustrated, or afraid? How will you express those emotions before they erupt into destructive anger?

2 How has anger affected your marriage? How can you and your spouse work to reduce anger's negative influence?

Y O U R   N O T E S / R E F L E C T I O N S / P R A Y E R S / G O A L S

_____

_____

_____

_____

_____

_____

_____

_____

_____

_____

_____

PASSION

15

Kiss me again and again, for your love is sweeter than wine. How fragrant your

cologne. . . . Take me with you. Come, let's run! Bring me into your bedroom.

Song of Songs 1:2-4

PRAYER

Lord, daily routines and unfulfilled expectations tend to dampen the fire that once burned in our relationship. Forgive us for taking each other for granted. Forgive us for letting the little things erode our affection. Help us to see our spouse with the fresh eyes of a lover, with eyes lit with passion. Give us insight to do the special, romantic things that make our relationship sparkle. Help us to be a couple that continues to eagerly look forward to being together. Amen.

SCRIPTURE

"Oh, feed me with your love . . . for I am utterly lovesick" (Song 2:5).

Charlotte Brontë defined passion well when she wrote, "I have found for the first time what I can truly love—I have found you. . . . A fervent, a solemn passion is conceived in my heart; it leans to you, draws you to my centre and spring of life, wraps my existence about you—and kindling in pure, powerful flame, fuses you and me in one."

Bill and I fell in love over a cup of hot tea in the college cafeteria thirty-one years ago. On Valentine's Day we decided we wanted to spend the rest of our lives together. That summer, on a warm August Montana evening (so the harvesters could get to the wedding), Bill and I pledged our lives to each other forever. We drove away toward San Francisco for our first jobs as youth pastor and church secretary, with scarcely a backward glance.

These were exciting, wonderful days: San Francisco, riding cable cars, having our own apartment, and dinner dates. They were what we called our "Velcro days." We were inseparable. We were in love. We were passionate. All we needed was each other.

And then, somewhere in the flurry of activity, reality began to sink in. The man began to irritate me. Oh, he was wonderful mostly, and we always kissed and made up after arguments. But I kept thinking, *As soon as I get him to be the way I want him, we'll once again have that exciting love, that passion . . . that Velcro feeling.* He had some irritating habits, like

never getting his socks in the hamper. He had to be on time—or early—everywhere we went. He was a man of order and liked to go to bed and get up at exactly the same time every day. He discovered, to his dismay, that the way I balanced a checkbook was to round it off to the nearest 10. On our budget, that was a disaster.

Many of you are probably like us. We all want to have a good marriage, to have the glow of love forever. We want to be intimate friends, lovers. But as I can tell from experience—it doesn't just happen. The process of staying in love, of being intimate friends and lovers must be constantly reevaluated, protected, and redefined.

No one really understands romance or sexual passion. Thousands of songs and poems have been written about its power and charm, evoking images of stars, the heavens, the wind, and a thousand other metaphors. Among those songs and poems is a biblical song "more wonderful than any other" (Song 1:1). The Song of Songs, written by Solomon to his lover, is a vivid expression of his love and passion. This wisest of men is obviously consumed by the magnetic chemistry of this love. When you read the Song, you see hot passion on every page.

What can we do to keep the passion fires burning in our marriages? While our popular culture would suggest that passion flows from sexy clothing and a well-honed physique, we suggest that passion is the result of many more foundational qualities and activities, like using good communication skills, showing appreciation, giving each other attention, learning to negotiate and compromise, practicing good personal hygiene, and getting rid of stress points. Add to these, attitudes of tenderness, loving surprises (flowers, unexpected notes, little gifts), spending time together in mutually enjoyable activities, and working from clearly defined roles and shared responsibility.

What will tend to dampen passion? Many things. Here are a few of the more common ones that many couples have shared with us: men who want sex without paying the price of good communication, women who nag, taking each other for granted, failing to maintain a "courtship" mentality, leaving unresolved arguments, poor hygiene, and stress of all kinds (money, in-laws, overcrowded schedules, etc.).

Of course, passion leads to sex. But sex, taken by itself, is nothing more than a biological function. For there to be good and mutually enjoyable sex, it must be within the context of a passionate romance. Yes, it is possible to keep passion alive, but it comes alive with intense caring.

Lord, you have given us to each other. Help us remember when our love was new and our passion was high. Give us new commitment to keep the passion alive in our relationship. As our love deepens, may our passion for the gift of marriage deepen as well. Rekindle the flame in us. Amen.

Passion

REFLECTION

"I love you ever and ever and without reserve. The more I have known you the more have I lov'd. . . . You are always new. The last of your kisses was ever the sweetest; the last smile the brightest; the last movement the gracefullest."

John Keats, quoted in *Quiet Moments for Couples*

"Romance is an attitude. It is a man and woman being alive to one another. . . . It is an atmosphere— a look that speaks more eloquently than words, a squeeze of the hand as you pass each other in a crowded room, a pat on the head or the shoulder for no particular reason. Romance is an element of fascination and delight that culminates in a deep desire to experience all of life with the one we love."

Joan Winmill Brown and Bill Brown, *Together Each Day*

LET'S TALK ABOUT IT

1 What hinders passion in your marriage? What encourages your passion to grow?

2 Discuss ways you and your spouse can rebuild and maintain passion for each other. Act on two of those ideas soon. Surprise your spouse with a romantic gesture within the next week.

YOUR NOTES/REFLECTIONS/PRAYERS/GOALS

_____

_____

_____

_____

_____

_____

_____

_____

_____

_____

_____

_____

_____

Passion

PURITY

16

The guilty walk a crooked path; the innocent travel a straight road.

Proverbs 21:8

PRAYER

Lord, I want to be faithful to the one person you have given me to be my life partner. I want to be faithful with my mind, with my emotions, and with my body. Help me keep my affections tuned in to the person with whom they belong. And help me never to let my body desecrate the vows to oneness that I have made before You. Amen.

SCRIPTURE

"God blesses those whose hearts are pure, for they will see God" (Matt. 5:8).

A young woman confessed to us that she was attracted to a married man. How could it be wrong, she wondered, when it felt so right? We told her what we have told dozens of others who have confessed a similar dilemma, that just because she was attracted to him didn't make it *right*. Noted scholar F. B. Meyer wrote, "Consecration is not an act of our feeling; but of our will." Feelings are not the litmus test of truth. It is God's Word alone that is true.

Frankly, people don't just wake up one day and fall helplessly into an affair. It happens back in our minds when we begin to fantasize about someone else or to be entertained by someone else's flirtations. The Bible calls this lust. Lust is the enemy of purity, and when it is left unchecked, it kindles dangerous emotions that become like an uncontrolled fire. F. B. Meyer is right. Remaining faithful, guarding the holy vows that you have made, and guarding your affection to one another are acts of the will. Those acts control our emotions.

Of course our resolve to be true to one another will be tested. What is a promise unless it is tested? Nothing but words. Many voices in our world speak directly against what we know is right. Our culture bombards us on all fronts to gratify ourselves, to fulfill ourselves. But as followers of Christ, we do not need to be afraid of testing. In fact, we can welcome it. Goethe wrote, "The absence of temptation is the absence of virtue."

It is not sin to be tempted. Jesus was tempted in all the ways that we are, and He understands us (Heb. 2:18). It is the response we make that determines whether or not that temptation turns to sin. James Dickey wrote, "We have all been in rooms we cannot die in." The point is not to stay in the room you don't belong in, not to dwell there, not to make it home. When we recognize a temptation from the enemy, it's time to get out of the room, to leave it.

In a midlife malaise David, the "man after God's own heart," looked next door and decided he knew best how to answer his own human hungers. He ended up in an adulterous relationship with Bathsheba. The subtle decision to do things his own way eventually led to murder to cover his tracks. His sin affected his household—his own life, the life of his family, his nation, and his relationship with God.

We all have moments of temptation to be unfaithful. Sexual sin happens in a sequence. First, we allow the temptation to linger. Next, because of the emotional pleasure of the fantasy, we begin to tell ourselves lies about the feelings. Then, the thoughts begin to germinate into an obsession. In the end we are nearly helpless to stop the sinful actions that will inevitably follow. This is not new. James said this centuries ago: "Temptation comes from the lure of our own evil desires. These evil desires lead to evil actions, and evil actions lead to death" (James 1:14–15).

Think *consequences.* Imagine what could happen if you did give in to your fantasies. Be realistic. Don't sugarcoat the consequences. Allow yourself to feel the painful emotions that such a disaster would bring.

If you are struggling with the concept of purity within your marriage, ask yourself some hard questions:

- Is it possible that I'm setting myself up for greater temptation by my lifestyle?
- Am I allowing an impure fantasy to linger in my mind?
- Am I flirting with danger by enjoying someone's flirtations toward me?
- Where are my weak points, my vulnerabilities, and how can I reinforce these areas?
- Do I need to increase accountability in my relationships or support systems that will give me balance in my life?

You can break the cycle of impurity at any stage if you will confess your temptation to God and then seek out someone who will guard your confidence and help you be accountable. The Bible says that when we sense we are being sucked into sin, we should "run from anything that stimulates youthful lust" (2 Tim. 2:22). You can overcome temptation. You can stay pure, even in a society that is sexually out of control and filled with obsessive lust. It is an act of your will, and God promises to be there if you will make the move in His direction.

Lord, we need you to be Lord of our sexuality. We want to be pure, first in our thoughts and then in our actions. When we are tempted, help us not to linger at the door of lustful fantasies but to run into your loving arms for protection and strength. In Jesus' name, amen.

REFLECTION

"Everyone needs to make some personal rules to live by. Life is just too complicated for us to succeed at living it unless we make some rules for ourselves. Not many of us are morally smart enough to wait until we actually run into a crisis before we make up our minds about what we ought to do in such a situation. There are too many crises and too many temptations for us to cope well with all of them without a game plan. We need to make some rules for ourselves, in advance."

Lewis Smedes, *Choices*

"In marriages, faithfulness is a symbol of commitment. It is a statement that our heart belongs to our spouse. This loyalty takes precedence over all other allegiances—parents, relatives, coworkers, and friends of each gender. Faithfulness insists that we allow no one to compete with this special place of affection."

Steve Stephens, *Experience the Best*

LET'S TALK ABOUT IT

1 What are the situations in which you are tempted? If you have fantasies that could lead to sexual impurity, commit them to God and ask Him for His help and strength. Find a friend who can hold you accountable.

2 How can you as spouses help each other stay pure?

YOUR NOTES/REFLECTIONS/PRAYERS/GOALS

_____

_____

_____

_____

_____

_____

_____

_____

_____

_____

_____

_____

_____

_____

Purity

EMOTIONAL
DIFFERENCES

17

O Lord, you have examined my heart and know everything about me. . . .

You know my every thought. . . . You know what I am going to say even before

I say it. . . . You watched me as I was being formed in utter seclusion. . . .

How precious are your thoughts about me, O God!

Psalm 139:1-2, 4, 15-17

PRAYER

Lord, help us to be willing to understand each other and respect one another's needs. You have said that if we truly love one another, we will stand our ground in defending each other. Thank You for reminding us that You are God and that You alone can meet the deep needs that we have. May both of us have a spirit of understanding and a commitment to pray for one another and our individual needs. Amen.

"Thank you for making me so wonderfully complex! Your workmanship is marvelous—and how well I know it" (Ps. 139:14).

INSIGHT

Gretchen and Eric married early and still had some growing up to do. They told us, "Our most difficult struggle is to accept one another as we are. We wanted so much from one another and were constantly disappointed." A turning point came at a retreat when Gretchen was challenged to thank God specifically for what He had given her. She began to thank God for Eric—even if he wasn't living up to her expectations. She began to look at him with different eyes, and he found it easier to change.

What are our emotional needs? Most of us feel the need to be truly loved, to be heard and understood, to be trusted, to be affirmed, to be emotionally vulnerable, and to be honest. Sometimes we need to be comforted. Other times we need to be encouraged. These are emotional needs a spouse can help to provide.

But it can be tempting to look to our spouse to fill all our emotional needs. However, that is not healthy. While each spouse certainly contributes to meeting the other's needs, neither can carry that responsibility alone. It is an impossible task. One of the dangers of looking exclusively to our spouse to meet our emotional needs is that we can fall into a par-

Emotional Differences

enting role with each other. We must remember that God created us to be partners, not parents, to our spouse.

What are your spouse's needs? What would your spouse say are his or her needs? What needs are realistic for you to meet?

Do you know what your emotional needs are? Does your spouse know what they are? Which needs are appropriate for your spouse to meet, and which ones are better met by other people?

Christina talked about some of the insights she's had about her emotional needs. "Jerry and I have been married for twelve years, and I only recently realized what a heavy set of expectations I have laid on him all these years. When I was honest with myself, I concluded that I looked to Jerry to be my primary listener, and while he is a good one, I always ended up being disappointed with him. I had a choice: I could be frustrated that my need to be heard was greater than Jerry's ability to listen, or I could find other ways to meet that need. I have recently started talking with one of the women from our church—a woman who verbally processes ideas the same way I do—and even though this woman and I do not talk about my marriage, my relationship to Jerry has become so much stronger because I have taken the pressure off him to be everything I need."

How willing are you to meet realistic needs your spouse has? If your spouse has a need for harmony and peace, are you willing to nip an argument in the bud by giving in—knowing where the argument has taken you a hundred times before? If you're like Bill and me, you tend to repeat the same arguments. You need to recognize that tendency and say, "I refuse to go there again. I know where this argument is headed. I'm going to give in and go a different direction this time." Instead you might ask, What does my spouse really need regarding this issue? How can I fill the need that is causing this repetitive argument? Ask God to help you see your spouse's point of view rather than continue to stay focused only on your own point of view.

If your spouse is stressed, are you willing to anticipate his or her needs before the stress pushes your spouse to the breaking point? Are you willing to help carry your spouse's load occasionally so that he or she can have an emotional respite?

One of the most important ways you can meet your spouse's emotional needs is by praying for him or her. If your spouse's need for love is greater than your capacity to love, pray that the Lord will provide other friends to fill the gap. If your spouse's need for affirmation is beyond your ability to fill, pray not only that God will make you more sensitive to your spouse's need but also that He will surround him or her with affirming people.

Lord, we thank You for teaching us what it means to truly love and accept one another for who we are. So often, Lord, we avoid seeing our spouse's needs because we are too insistent on voicing our own. Give us not only the courage to discover our spouse's real needs but also the willingness and strength to do what we can to meet them. Then help us trust You to do the rest. In Jesus' name, amen.

REFLECTION

"Conflict is not something tragic, or to be feared, or to run from. It is a normal part of any close relationship. It is in fact raw material to be worked on and transmuted into an opportunity to grow. A conflict may even be welcomed, because it pinpoints an area where an adjustment has to be made. . . . Couples who learn to work on their conflicts . . . are continually improving their relationship. . . . Each conflict resolved marks another milestone in their progress toward relationship."

David Mace, *Love and Anger in Marriage*

"If you have needs that are unmet, instead of making demands or accusations, try to meet the needs of your marriage partner. Love begets love; resentment begets hostility; rejection begets rejection."

Cecil Osborne, *The Art of Understanding Your Mate*

LET'S TALK ABOUT IT

1 What are your greatest emotional needs? Are these needs your spouse can help meet? Are you being fair to ask your spouse to meet these needs, or are these needs that only God can meet?

2 Compare notes with your spouse and ask how you can help meet your spouse's needs.

YOUR NOTES/REFLECTIONS/PRAYERS/GOALS

_____

_____

_____

_____

_____

_____

_____

_____

_____

_____

_____

_____

PRAYING FOR THE PRESENCE OF GOD IN OUR SPIRITUAL DEVELOPMENT

Spiritual Unity

Forgiveness

Commitments

Study of God's Word

Worship

PART 4

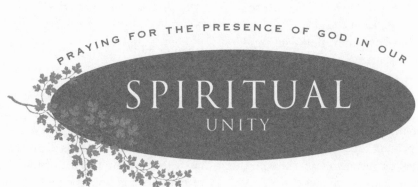

PRAYING FOR THE PRESENCE OF GOD IN OUR

SPIRITUAL
UNITY

18

That all of them may be one, Father, just as you are in me and I am in you.

John 17:21, NIV

PRAYER

Lord, we know that You have created us to be "one flesh" despite our very real differences. How we long to be of one mind, one heart, one spirit, yet so often we are not united in spirit. First of all, may we love and honor You as individuals. Then teach us to walk together with You, knowing that the closer we are to You, the closer we will be to each other. In Jesus' name, amen.

SCRIPTURE

"Together you are the body of Christ. Each one of you is part of his body" (1 Cor. 12:27, CEV).

Shortly after Bill and I were married, we were at a missions convention, and the speaker's compassion for non-Christians deeply moved us. We wanted to give all that we were, all that we had, to God. After the service, we knelt together at the altar, dedicating our lives to God's purposes. Both Bill and I look back to that place as an unusual time when we were united in spirit to do God's will. We have had similar times of sensing God's touch and calling, of pulling together spiritually. Sometimes in the ordinary moments of praying together or reading Scripture together, we feel that we are on the same spiritual page.

But other times we feel as if we live on completely different spiritual planets. Like most couples, we are very different from one another. Life pressures encroach, and we drift apart spiritually.

A personal relationship with God is by nature intensely private, yet within a Christian marriage, it is a joint pursuit, too. How can we have spiritual unity when we men and women are so different from one another? How can we experience unity when we grow at different rates? Spiritual unity within marriage is an area that can hold a lot of unmet expectations and misunderstanding.

If we are truly to be "one flesh," how do we invite God's presence into our marriage? As Bill and I have learned to pull back and have

respect for the God-shaped vacuum that only He can fill in the other, we are drawn closer together in our spiritual journeys. It is freeing to realize that God does not deal with us according to some prescribed manner or code.

Keep in mind two important factors in keeping spiritual unity within your marriage:

Show respect for what God is doing in your spouse. My idea of how God should be working in my spouse may be quite different from God's actual plan. Nothing kills a spiritual quest faster than nagging or preaching. An attitude of humility and honesty helps genuine spiritual unity.

Many women we surveyed were frustrated over the fact that their husbands were not spiritual leaders. Keri's comment was typical: "Our spiritual desires are at much different levels, and this has been a constant challenge. I get tired of being the one to initiate spiritual activity." Keri can show respect for what God is doing in her husband's life by working on her listening skills and allowing her husband to grow at his own pace. Sometimes in our eagerness to share what God is doing in our own lives, we can overwhelm our spouse by insisting we go to church every time the doors are open or expecting him or her to live up to some invisible standard.

Valerie's situation is common, too. She has been married twenty years. Her husband is not a believer and shows no interest in spiritual matters. She said, "My husband thinks I'm a Bible-thumper and doesn't like it when I read spiritual books. He doesn't understand my wanting to pursue God at all." Valerie often feels frustrated and spiritually alone, but as she is waiting on God for her husband's salvation, she is learning to be patient.

God is a personal God. You—not your spouse—will stand before God and give an account for your life. If your spouse is not interested in the things of God, work on your own relationship with God while continuing to love your spouse. The only love that will never disappoint you is God's love, and it is a pursuit to be highly treasured, regardless of our spouse's response to God.

Make a conscious effort to commit time and energy to pursue God together. If your spouse is a Christian, do the two of you make room for God in your relationship? Take time to pray together, to read the Bible together, and to discuss your spiritual journey. Your spouse, the person who knows you the best, can be your greatest partner in understanding God's will in your life and in serving Him.

You will bring God's presence into your marriage if pursuing Him is at the core of your life. What is at the core of your marriage? Is it children, work, church, social life, extended family, sports? How can you make your spiritual growth and unity the center of your relationship?

The challenges of life—work, raising a family, and all the extra demands—deeply affect the spiritual condition of our marriages. There are times one of us may be going through a "dark night of the soul," a time of questioning God. This is no time to give up. It's a time more than ever to wait on God and to avoid pat answers. This is the place to turn to Him—the true source of everything. Difficulties and tests are gifts to propel us *together* into His presence, to remind us that knowing God is the most important unifying factor of our lives.

Lord, I love You with all my heart and pledge to make knowing You the highest calling of my life. Forgive me for spiritual pride, for thinking You must deal with my spouse in a certain way. I trust You with my spouse's spiritual walk. May both of us approach this area with the greatest of humility and honesty. In Jesus' name, amen.

REFLECTION

"God's intention for marriage is to grow or subdue each partner in relation to the other in order to draw each—and eventually the marriage itself—to reflect the character of his Son."

Dan B. Allender and Tremper Longman III, *Intimate Allies*

"We realize that no earthly love, no matter how wonderful and intimate and beautiful, can replace our need for closeness to God. He has created us so that there is a place within which we can be satisfied only by intimate fellowship with Him. In the shelter of His love, our love for one another can safely grow and flower until it is transformed by heaven into something even more wonderful."

C. S. Lewis, *The Great Divorce*

LET'S TALK ABOUT IT

1. After prayerful consideration, privately list your own top three spiritual goals.

2. Later, share them with your spouse and discuss why you think they are important. Together, agree on one spiritual goal you both desire, and discuss how you can attain it.

YOUR NOTES/REFLECTIONS/PRAYERS/GOALS

_____

_____

_____

_____

_____

_____

_____

_____

_____

_____

PRAYING FOR THE PRESENCE OF GOD IN OUR

FORGIVENESS

19

So if you are standing before the altar . . . and you suddenly remember that

someone has something against you, leave your sacrifice there beside the altar.

Go and be reconciled to that person. Then come and offer your sacrifice to God.

Matthew 5:23-24

PRAYER

Lord, how natural and powerful is the urge to keep score, to remember the slights, the wrongs, the little irritants that often grow. We know this is a self-centered habit that can ruin the love, joy, and unity You intend for our marriage to have. Forgive us, Lord, for not forgiving, when You so freely offer forgiveness to us. Help us to let go of the past, to truly forgive. In Jesus' name, amen.

SCRIPTURE

"You must make allowance for each other's faults and forgive the person who offends you. Remember, the Lord forgave you, so you must forgive others" (Col. 3:13).

INSIGHT

Not long ago Bill and I were sitting around a table with several other couples, reminiscing. We began sharing stories from some of the most difficult times in our marriages, and in this time of honest sharing, it was amazing to see how hurts of the past were still powerful, still there. One of the couples—now deeply committed to love one another—told us of a seemingly impossible time when they nearly separated. To look at them now, one would never know they could easily have been a divorce statistic. What held their marriage together? *Forgiveness.* They were able to confess their sin to each other, to extend forgiveness, and to allow the forgiveness to heal their pain. As we talked, all of us were reminded how essential forgiveness is because of the great potential there is in every marriage for wounds.

Jesus spent a lot of time teaching about forgiveness. At one point Peter asked Him, "Lord, how often should I forgive someone who sins against me? Seven times?"

"No!" Jesus replied, "seventy times seven!" (Matt 18:21-22). Then He went on to tell the story of a man who couldn't pay his debt of millions of dollars and who begged for mercy from the king. The king had pity on

the man and forgave his debt. But when the shoe was on the other foot and a fellow servant owed the man a smaller debt, he had the servant arrested. The king heard about it and had the first man sent to prison until he had paid every penny. In other words, we do not receive forgiveness if we do not forgive.

We disappoint and fail one another every day in our marriages. Sometimes we grievously sin against one another. How important it is, then, for us to *live* forgiveness. *Knowing* we should forgive and *doing* it are two separate actions. But we can be glad that God promises to give us the strength to forgive. We can forgive our spouse only because God in his love has first forgiven us.

If we ignore each other's sin or if we fail to forgive, our individual lives and our marriage will be deeply affected. Resisting the need to forgive leads to bitterness. The Bible warns us, "Watch out that no bitterness takes root among you, for as it springs up it causes deep trouble, hurting many in their spiritual lives" (Heb. 12:15, TLB).

What is a root of bitterness? Roots are an efficient network that feeds the plant, making it grow. Some roots, especially young ones, come out easily when pulled. But then there are those stubborn ones that go deep, strong. They are the ones that have been allowed to flourish, that have been fed. When bitterness comes between a husband and wife, it can be nasty stuff. Bitterness needs to be addressed, or the marriage will be in trouble. How important it is in marriage to keep short accounts. Yes, we are offended by one another. Yes, we sin against each other. But it's essential to recognize our sin, confess it to each other, forgive each other, and let it go. If we do not, unforgiveness and bitterness can poison our lives.

We need grace to forgive each other. Grace and forgiveness are not one-time actions. We need them every day, just like food. Awareness of our own need for grace helps us give grace to our spouse.

Commit yourself to forgiving your spouse. Look inside yourself to see if you are secretly nursing old wounds or grudges against your spouse. Dredge them up and offer them to God, asking Him to give you the grace to forgive. Look inside yourself again to see if you are causing bitterness or resentment in your spouse. Identify ways that you have sinned against your spouse. Then take time to confess those sins to your spouse and ask for his or her forgiveness.

Forgiveness is complex. Don't wait to try to have it all make sense before you open your arms to forgive and be forgiven. In his book *As for Me and My House,* Walter Wangerin writes, "Forgiveness is a Divine absurdity. Forgiveness is a holy, complete, unqualified giving." And it is the balm that heals and restores.

Lord, how easy it is within marriage to let anger harden into unforgiveness and bitterness that drives a wedge between us. Give me the courage to look at my sin against my spouse and confess it. Give me the grace to forgive when my spouse sins against me. I pray that we will be people who choose to forgive and love each other, because I know that is Your plan for us. Amen.

Forgiveness

REFLECTION

"What do I do when I forgive? I surrender my right to hurt back. I lay down the axe just as I am about to bring it crashing down on the head of my enemy. And I do it for one reason only: God has asked me to. In return, he offers me the greatest gift anyone can know—to be at peace with the Creator of the universe and the Master of our souls. This is a more powerful stress reliever than any tranquilizer or blood pressure medicine. I know, because I've tasted it myself!"

Archibald Hart, *Adrenaline and Stress*

"Vengeance is having a videotape planted in your soul that cannot be turned off. It plays the painful scene over and over again inside your mind. It hooks you into its instant replays. And each time it replays, you feel the clap of pain again. Is it fair? Forgiving turns off the videotape of pained memory. Forgiving sets you free. Forgiving is the only way to stop the cycle of unfair pain turning in your memory."

Lewis Smedes, *Forgiveness*

LET'S TALK ABOUT IT

1 What do you need to confess to your spouse? When forgiveness is extended, allow it to heal the wound.

2 If your spouse has seriously wronged you, write out the "wrong" in detail on a piece of paper. Then pray, "Lord, I give this to You, the perfect judge. I trust You with the outcome." At a convenient time, share this with your spouse, and if possible, together burn the piece of paper in the fireplace. When you are tempted to relive this offense, remember that it has been burned—it is in God's hands, not yours.

YOUR NOTES/REFLECTIONS/PRAYERS/GOALS

_____

_____

_____

_____

_____

_____

_____

_____

COMMITMENTS

20

Love never gives up, never loses faith, is always hopeful, and endures

through every circumstance.

1 Corinthians 13:7

PRAYER

Lord, how easy it is to want to live life according to our own whims and wants. Thank You for showing us in Your Word what it means to be loyal and true to our vows and the important principles that shape our lives. Give us the courage to resist our culture's pull to fulfill ourselves at the cost of our commitments, knowing Your righteous and true ways are best. Amen.

SCRIPTURE

"The Lord is not slack concerning His promise, as some count slackness, but is longsuffering toward us, not willing that any should perish" (2 Pet. 3:9, NKJV).

The woman on the plane beside me (Nancie) was talking to her friend in the seat next to her. I couldn't help overhearing their animated conversation. She wanted out of her boring marriage and complained to her friend, "There's just no joy in it any more."

The friend encouraged her to leave her husband and said, "Look, honey, if you're not in it for *you,* get out!"

I wanted to interrupt and say, "Oh, but a committed marriage is for you!" Of course we don't always feel like keeping commitments—which is exactly why we need them. To be committed means to order our lives around principles bigger than our immediate feelings and wants. And next to our commitment to God, the commitment of marriage is the most sacred and binding commitment most of us will make. And within that commitment—in spite of the "boring" and tedious parts of it—is a gift that offers security, definition, and the base from which we raise children and live our lives.

We see all around us the crumbling of our society, symptomatic of the crumbling of important commitments. Marriage is a foundational commitment that holds our families, churches, communities, and nation together. Psalm 11:3 reminds us, "If the foundations are destroyed, what can the righteous do?" (NKJV).

I found myself wanting to join the conversation and tell my two seatmates about Charles

and Elizabeth, a couple in their early sixties in our small town. Elizabeth has been deteriorating with a muscular ailment, but every day Charles takes her out for a walk in her wheelchair, and her face is wreathed in smiles to feel the sunshine on her face and to have her husband with her. Every spring they do laps to raise money for the local chapter of Young Life. Ask Charles if he's ever bored, having to feed his wife now and take care of her basic needs. What has held him to Elizabeth? Commitment, and it is beautiful to watch.

I began to think of so many couples who have held together through the years, for better and for worse. I thought of the day more than thirty years ago when Bill and I pledged our lives to one another in my home church in Conrad, Montana. We really had no idea what it meant to love one another "for better, for worse; for richer, for poorer; in sickness, and in health." That commitment we made to one another has had a lifelong impact. Has it always been exciting and wonderful? Of course not. We have had to have commitment to have stayed married! There have been boring times, frustrating times. We also realize that for some couples, dire circumstances cause them to break their commitment—they are victims of divorce. And the pain it causes is exponential because the shredding of this commitment affects so many.

It's important to understand that it is going against the tide of our culture to be in a committed marriage. In their influential book

Commitments

Habits of the Heart, Dr. Robert Bellah and his colleagues from UCLA concluded that many Americans don't believe in commitment anymore. The higher ethic we subscribe to is every individual's right to be satisfied with life and every individual's right to pursue his or her own fulfillment. This belief often clashes with being committed to someone who lacks the power to bring us the satisfaction we think we deserve.

Bill and I have found that we need the presence of God in our lives to stay committed. Over time, we've come to realize that if we are true to our primary commitment of loving God and obeying His Word, it's easier to keep our other important commitments. We can follow His example because Jesus has made commitments to us. He committed His very life to us and made these promises in His word: "I will never leave you nor forsake you" (Heb. 13:5, NKJV); "I will come again" (John 14:3, NKJV).

The most important and sacred things in life require protecting, and that means we must be proactive in protecting our commitment to our marriage. We protect it by putting our heart into our marriage and by truly being present to our commitment. In his book *Caring and Commitment,* Lewis Smedes writes about what it means to make a commitment to someone: "I stretch myself into unpredictable days ahead, and I will be a small island of certainty in the swirling waters of uncertainties." To be committed to someone is to be there for them, no matter what.

Lord, thank You for Your precious commitment to us, to love us through life, giving us security and peace. We pray that we will grasp more fully this crucial aspect of love—the quality of commitment. May we have a "stubborn love" that will hold through time and circumstances. Amen.

REFLECTION

"There are a lot of marriages today that break up just at the point where they could mature and deepen. We are taught to quit when it hurts. But often, it is the times of pain that produce the most growth in a relationship."

Madeleine L'Engle, *The Door Interviews*

"All couples struggle; all couples need God's transforming power. And every couple—even those whose marriages have been difficult from the start—share the biggest, most glaring road sign of the marriage experience: their wedding vows. God goes to great lengths to honor the vows made between men and women."

Paul Kortepeter, "Ridin' on the Freeway of Love"

1 Discuss your five most important commitments and how they shape your marriage.

2 How can you build in safeguards to protect these commitments?

YOUR NOTES/REFLECTIONS/PRAYERS/GOALS

_____

_____

_____

_____

_____

_____

_____

_____

_____

_____

_____

_____

_____

_____

_____

Commitments

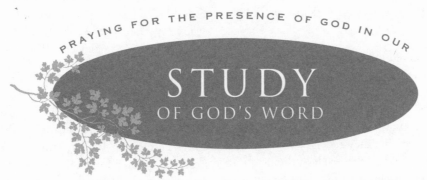

PRAYING FOR THE PRESENCE OF GOD IN OUR

STUDY
OF GOD'S WORD

21

Your word is a lamp for my feet and a light for my path.

Psalm 119:105

PRAYER

Lord, You alone have the words of eternal life. You also have the words of blessing, love, and power that I desperately need in my everyday life. All these are included in Your holy Word. Help me to seek Your Word first for answers and wisdom. May I delight in the knowledge and counsel contained in Scripture. I commit to reading Your holy Word, and I thank You for giving me this precious and life-giving revelation. Amen.

SCRIPTURE

"My heart stands in awe of Your word. I rejoice at Your word as one who finds great treasure"
(Ps. 119:161-162, NKJV).

Discovering the power of God's Word together can strengthen a marriage in significant ways. But like most couples, Bill and I struggled with how we could study the Bible together in our hectic lives when we were doing well just to have our personal Bible study time.

We were inspired by watching our friends Gene and Marylou. Even though they frequently are separated by time and schedules, they read the same passages of Scripture in their private devotions. Later, they share with one another insights they received from their reading. They told us that each of them often sees the same passage with different perspectives. Their study together delights them and is enhancing the power of God's Word in their marriage. Bill and I are doing the same thing and finding a fresh love for God's Word *together*.

In their book *How Can We Be Sure Our Marriage Will Last?*, Charlie and Martha Shedd, married forty-seven years, relate how they first began to realize the strength they gleaned from Bible study together. "We made a commitment. Every day we would read the Bible together. We would agree on a book, and then we would take turns reading one chapter to each other . . . every day. How did that go? It didn't. . . . Because we were not synchronized in those early morning hours, we would have our quiet times at different hours. And we still do. Every day for forty years,

we've read our Bibles and had our quiet times, each at our own time. Every week for two thousand-eighty weeks, we've come together (at least once) for sharing, 'What did the Lord say this week to you, to me, for us together?' The more we are faithful to Bible study together, the better our marriage goes . . . the better *everything* goes."

Another couple we know reads the Bible together every morning at breakfast, before they leave for their jobs. They use a book that allows them to read through the entire New Testament, Psalms, and Proverbs in a year. They have found that reading Scripture together anchors them as they begin their day and helps them focus their prayer time on God's character as it was revealed in that day's reading.

Why should we study the Bible? Bible reading is important because through it we come to know the character of God and how to live in this world. Reading the Bible not only shows us Christ but also increases our faith. Romans 10:17 reminds us, "So then faith comes by hearing, and hearing by the word of God" (NKJV). Ongoing study of the Bible keeps us balanced, constantly reminding us of who God is when we lose perspective.

Sometimes we can be intimidated by the idea of studying the Bible, but there is no perfect time or method. The important thing is to begin. Start by choosing a version of the

Study of God's Word

Bible that you can easily understand. (A great one to begin with is the New Living Translation.) Then begin reading a chapter or two at a time, taking care to think and reflect on what you read. Ask as you read, "What does this passage or this story say to us?"

Share with your spouse what you are learning from Scripture—not in a preachy way, but in an honest way that tells your spouse how God's Word is comforting you or leading you. When you or your spouse is grappling with a difficult issue, the other spouse can share Scripture passages that may give direction or encouragement. Find a wonderful promise from God's Word and slip it into your spouse's suitcase or lunch bag. Bill and I have also found it helpful to write out on note cards specific verses that speak to us about certain issues in our lives.

A small-group Bible study with other couples can also help you grow together in your understanding of God's Word. Your church may even offer such a group. Check out a Christian bookstore for other books and studies that can help you learn from the Bible.

God's Word is the guiding principle for our lives, and how essential it is to take time to study it, to reflect on our lives to see if they fit His design. God has a carefully designed plan for us, and His Word will guide us and become the driving force of our lives. Proverbs 4:26 says, "Ponder the path of thy feet, and let all thy ways be established" (KJV). A study of God's Word helps us ponder our own paths, to be thoughtful about how we are living our lives.

Lord, we praise You for the wonderful treasure of Your Word. We pray for a sense of creativity and commitment to help us find ways to center our lives on Your Word. Give us the courage to read with open hearts and minds and to be willing to measure our lives against Your truth, to be willing to change. Give us tenacity to seek Your truth. Amen.

Study of God's Word

REFLECTION

"The Bible is like a telescope. If a man looks through his telescope, then he sees worlds beyond; but if he looks at his telescope, then he does not see anything but that. The Bible is a thing to be looked through, to see that which is beyond; but most people only look at it; and so they only see the dead letter."

Phillips Brooks, quoted in *Treasury of the Christian Faith*

"It is one of the spiritual tragedies of our times that in taking the historical and literary dimensions of the Bible, we have neglected it as the book of life. We need now to spend less time in measuring the Bible, and more time in allowing the Bible to measure us."

Walter Calvert, quoted in *Treasury of the Christian Faith*

LET'S TALK ABOUT IT

1 How can you strengthen your marriage by learning to love and obey God's Word? Consider what you need to do to study God's Word together on a more consistent basis.

2 Share with your spouse today something that has changed in your life as a result of reading and hearing Scripture that penetrated to your heart.

YOUR NOTES/REFLECTIONS/PRAYERS/GOALS

_____

_____

_____

_____

_____

_____

_____

_____

_____

_____

_____

Study of God's Word

PRAYING FOR THE PRESENCE OF GOD IN OUR

WORSHIP

22

Lord, I have loved the habitation of Your house,

and the place where Your glory dwells.

Psalm 26:8, NKJV

PRAYER

Almighty God, we worship You. You are Lord of the universe, all-powerful and altogether righteous! Be Lord of our lives and our marriage. You are the Creator of all things, and we give You praise. As a couple we submit our lives and our marriage to You. May our actions and words be pleasing to You. Amen.

SCRIPTURE

"Come, let us worship and bow down. Let us kneel before the Lord our maker, for he is our God. We are the people he watches over, the sheep under his care. Oh, that you would listen to his voice today!" (Ps. 95:6-7).

When I think of worshiping together, my immediate thoughts are of being in church with Bill, singing praises to God, giving honor to His name, and studying the Word through a sermon. But worship is far more than going to church or mere words or phrases. Worship is a heart response.

Think back to when you and your spouse were first in love. You "worshiped" each other, in a sense. The object of your desire and love consumed your heart and thoughts.

That's the kind of worship God wants from us. He wants our hearts and thoughts to be consumed by His presence. He wants us to desire Him intensely. "Oh, that they would always have hearts like this, that they might fear me and obey all my commands! If they did, they and their descendants would prosper forever" (Deut. 5:29). God knows that to worship Him—our Creator—is right for us.

We are created with an innate desire to worship. As songwriter Bob Dylan sings, "You've got to serve somebody. . . . It may be the devil or it may be the Lord, but you got to serve somebody!" We worship that which becomes most important in our lives. Whatever or whomever we honor above all else with our time, money, and energy is indeed what we worship. Worship is symbolic of our first love.

But our hearts can be fickle. We can often be like the children of Israel. When they got bored waiting for Moses to return from his long visit with God on Mount Sinai, they created a golden calf to worship (Exod. 32). They decided that they needed to be able to *see* the object of their worship. But God's Word is very clear about the object of our worship: "You shall fear the Lord your God and serve Him, and shall take oaths in His name. You shall not go after other gods, the gods of the peoples who are all around you" (Deut. 6:13-14, NKJV).

Why are we here on this earth? Our chief purpose is to glorify God. We are here to praise, honor, and serve Him. Sometimes we get it backward and think that God is here to *serve us*—and our prayers show it. And God becomes the mere source of energy for carrying on our activities rather than the One whom we seek. While church attendance does not take the place of real worship, it is indicative of where our hearts are and it often is the place where our hearts are opened to worship. The simple commitment of worshiping God with other believers brings strength and a sense of purpose to our lives. We worship through taking communion, while remembering what the ceremony means. Worshipful music in our homes and cars, personal devotions, and family prayers are acts of worship to help make real what we know—that He alone is worthy of all our praise.

Many couples that we surveyed pointed to a turning point in their lives spiritually when they committed themselves to worship together consistently, giving back, not just taking. Worshiping God together with His people is an undeniable strength and unifier to couples. As Bob and Linda said, "It took a family crisis to make us realize that we had not been consistent with going to church or having family worship. We were devastated by the crisis, but it took us in the right direction with God. We're doing so much better."

Worship cannot be forced. Worship is an act of our will, springing from our hearts, a choice to praise and honor God—to give Him our best. Worship pulls us to the real agenda: That God is great and is worthy of our praise.

Hundreds of years ago, Thomas à Kempis wrote in *The Imitation of Christ*, "It is a great thing to live in obedience for we are too much ruled by our own passions." We obey God by worshiping Him—our first love—seven days a week.

Commit yourself to worshiping with your spouse, allowing those times not only to cement your relationship to God but also to make a statement to yourself and others that God is the Lord of your life. One couple described their time in church together as an intimately spiritual time. "Sometimes when the congregation is singing a song that speaks of God's love, Matt and I find ourselves overcome to the point of tears, especially if one of us has had a hard week. It's as if God is speaking to us through the words of our singing, healing the hurts and restoring us. Those times of worship are priceless."

Lord, we say we want to worship You above all else, but other things crowd in. It can be easy to neglect times of corporate and family worship. Help us not to put selfish priorities over You. Remind us that in worshiping You together, we are making a powerful statement of who You are to us. And we affirm: You are Lord! Amen.

R E F L E C T I O N

"There are two reasons for loving God: no one is more worthy of our love, and no one can return more in response to our love. God deserves our love because He first loved us. His love for us was genuine because He sought nothing for Himself."

Bernard of Clairvaux, *On Loving God*

"No love of the natural heart is safe unless the human heart has been satisfied by God first."

Oswald Chambers, *He Shall Glorify Me*

LET'S TALK ABOUT IT

1 How can you and your spouse place a higher priority on worshiping God together?

2 How does your life reflect what is most important to you? A look at your checkbook and calendar may give you some clues.

YOUR NOTES/REFLECTIONS/PRAYERS/GOALS

_____

_____

_____

_____

_____

_____

_____

_____

_____

_____

_____

_____

_____

Worship

PRAYING FOR THE PRESENCE OF GOD IN OUR SHARED PRIORITIES

PART 5

Putting God First

Making Wise Choices

Purpose for Living

Goals

Handling Money

Managing Time

Sharing Work

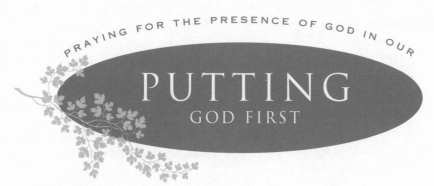

PUTTING
GOD FIRST

23

In everything you do, put God first, and he will direct you

and crown your efforts with success.

Proverbs 3:6, TLB

PRAYER

Lord, give us the wisdom to put You first in our lives. We want our two hearts not only to beat as one but also to beat with Your heart. Give us the will to follow You, the courage to want to see life and others as You do. Give us individually and together hearts to be obedient to You in every way. Amen.

SCRIPTURE

"Honor the Lord with your wealth and with the best part of everything" (Prov. 3:9).

The Page family seems to have it all. Both David and Judy have rewarding jobs with good salaries. They have excellent childcare for their three-year-old. They have a new home, a new Jeep Cherokee for hauling their boat on weekend outings, and a membership in the local golf country club. They go to a large church with great worship music and inspirational sermons. One thing they like about their church is that they can go to the early service, be in and out in about an hour, and still have time to do other recreational activities. They can also miss a Sunday now and then, and nobody really notices.

Putting God First

Judy is expecting their second child in four months. In spite of all that they have, Judy has this gnawing feeling that something is missing. She feels an undercurrent of discontent. Her doctor says she is mildly depressed. She finds herself asking why she should feel this way when she has a wonderful husband and the perfect life.

Judy admits that as much as she and Dave have, they always seem to want more. They have little desire for growing deeper with God, and Judy knows this is wrong. "Why don't I want to seek God instead of always buying more things?" she sighs. Judy and Dave are not unlike many Christian couples. The Pages have a problem with the order of their priorities.

In our self-sufficient world, it is easy to *attach* God to our life as a part of the whole. He becomes the God we underline in our Bibles, the God of provision and promises, but not the Lord God Almighty. Making God a *part of our lives* and having Him as *Lord of our lives* are two quite different things. In the swirling water of this life, nothing is stable other than the Solid Rock. Putting God first is the only way to build a strong foundation for our marriage.

So, you may ask, How do we actually put God first? Here are some things to consider:

Recognize the difference between your "source" and your "means." We often confuse our bank accounts, educational degrees, abilities, and influential contacts as our source of provision and blessing. However, these are simply the means by which God, the Source, provides for us. God uses the material resources of this life as the delivery system to care for those of us who trust Him. But He is our true Source.

Give God your "firstfruits." Many wonderful passages in the Bible talk about giving God the firstfruits of our life. "The first of the firstfruits of your land you shall bring into the house of the Lord your God" (Exod. 23:19, NKJV). In Old Testament times, the firstfruits were the first pickings of a harvest or the first animals of a flock or a herd. Today we think of firstfruits a bit differently. They are simply the first—most important—portion of our time and resources. Giving God our firstfruits simply means that He has priority. Some couples express that God comes first by writing out the check for His work as the first one each week. Other couples emphasize that it is important to give back to God in time. They volunteer for various ministries in their church and like to reach out to others in need, not because they get something for it, but because they want to put God's agenda first.

Spend quality time, not just token time, with God. We face so many demands on our time that it is easy to put aside a silent God who does not scream for our attention. But God is not in a hurry, and He will never shout. Nancie and I find that we consciously have to set aside time to be in God's presence. Otherwise, we end up praying token prayers, quickies that make us feel less guilt. We have to be patient, take time to listen, spend time reading His Word if we are to really know Him and make Him first in our life. Someone has said that we are a generation that wants

"truth in a nutshell, depth in a hurry." However, that's not the way God operates.

Choose friends who draw you closer to God. The other couples you spend time with are a key to putting God first. Choose couples who share your desire to let Him be first. You can then have a positive influence on each other and strengthen each other's priorities.

Does this mean that you give up your dream for a better life? Not at all. It simply means that you have put your life in the order that God intends so that He can bless you and maximize your opportunities. It may require some sacrifice on your part along the way, but ultimately it will produce a most satisfying life.

Lord, help us to not get trapped into trying to make heaven here on earth. Help us to avoid greed, covetousness, and the constant pursuit of more amenities. Help us to be willing to sacrifice all for your glory. In Jesus' name, amen.

REFLECTION

"The Christian life is the life of Christ reproduced in the believer by the power of the Holy Spirit in obedient response to the Word of God. It is the incredible blend of supernatural power transfused into an ordinary life. What is the best laboratory in which to develop this remarkable life? Perhaps the most realistic test site is marriage. The highest highs and the lowest lows are likely to happen there."

Howard and Jeanne Hendricks, *Husbands and Wives*

"It is part of our fallen nature to want to control each other rather than sacrificially to serve one another as an act of love. Competition for first place, the right to rule the roost, threatens the health of any marriage. When we submit ourselves to the Lord Jesus Christ, however, competition turns into loving empathy."

Wayne Oates, quoted in *Husbands and Wives*

. . . .   101

LET'S TALK ABOUT IT

1 Be brutally honest. What are your priorities? What do you need to change in order to put God in first place?

2 Discuss with each other what it means to put God first, with your finances, time, hobbies, family, and marriage. Let the Holy Spirit guide you as you ponder these important aspects of ordering your priorities.

YOUR NOTES/REFLECTIONS/PRAYERS/GOALS

_____

_____

_____

_____

_____

_____

_____

_____

_____

_____

_____

_____

_____

PRAYING FOR THE PRESENCE OF GOD IN OUR

MAKING
WISE CHOICES

24 . . . .

Anyone who listens to my teaching and obeys me is wise, like a person who builds a

house on solid rock. Though the rain comes in torrents and the floodwaters rise and

the winds beat against that house, it won't collapse, because it is built on rock.

Matthew 7:24-25

PRAYER

Lord, we acknowledge our need for your wisdom in all aspects of our lives. We want to make good choices in the use of the time and resources you have entrusted to us. Teach us to rely on the sound judgment that comes from You rather than on our emotional impulses. Help us to be "wise as serpents and gentle as doves." In Jesus' name, amen.

"Anyone who hears my teaching and ignores it is foolish, like a person who builds a house on sand. When the rains and floods come and the winds beat against that house, it will fall with a mighty crash" (Matt. 7:26-27).

INSIGHT

One of the not-so-smart investments I (Bill) ever made was purchasing some stock on a "hot" tip from a broker. This broker, whom I had never met, said the stock was a "slam dunk" and those who got in on the ground floor would be rich. Without praying, without consulting Nancie, and without educating myself further about this company, I bought several hundred shares of this stock on the enthusiasm of this broker and his sales pitch. I bought the stock at eight dollars per share, and within weeks the stock had dropped to three dollars per share. A year later, the stock was worth ten cents per share, and the broker had been indicted for fraud. This was not just bad luck. I made some fundamental mistakes. Had I made the choice wisely, I would have gone through the following steps:

Take your time; beware of your impulse. Most of us have made impulsive decisions as the result of high-pressure sales pitches. We know that emotional, impulsive decisions are often the wrong decisions, mainly because they do not give us time to think and to listen to God speak. Usually the opportunity will wait, and if it won't wait, it may not be God's will for us anyway.

Do some homework and educate yourself. Both you and your spouse should gather good information in order to make good choices. Jesus gave graphic examples of the wisdom of this approach. He said, "Who would begin construction of a building without first getting estimates and then checking to see if there is enough money to pay the bills? Otherwise, you might complete only the foundation before running out of funds. And then how everyone would laugh at you! . . . Or what king would ever dream of going to war without first sitting down with his counselors and discussing whether his army of ten thousand is strong enough to defeat the twenty thousand soldiers who are marching against him?" (Luke 14:28-31).

Decisions about going to work for a particular company, choosing a church, buying a home, purchasing a car, investing your savings, and even choosing a pet should be done with as much information as possible. It is impossible to make wise and informed decisions without enough information.

Pray about the decision before you make it. Too often we make a decision and then ask God

Making Wise Choices

to bless it. (I confess that is what I did with the stock purchase I mentioned earlier!) This does not leave room for God to alter our choices or change our mind.

Make mutual decisions. It is selfish and even insulting to our spouse to make major decisions without discussing them together first. Our spouse can give us valuable perspective. Some people may hesitate to ask their spouse's opinion because they already know the answer is not the one they want to hear. But part of marriage is being one, not only in flesh, but also of one mind. The choices that Nancie and I have made together, after discussion, prayer, and adequate information, have turned out to be the best ones we have made. Proverbs reminds us, "Don't go ahead with your plans without the advice of others" (Prov. 20:18, TLB).

Sometimes marriage partners will have to compromise or say no to a choice if they can't agree. A good marriage is one of compromise. We do not always get our way in a marriage, and decisions that are not mutual will ultimately lead to discord and discontent.

Guard your love of stuff. In an affluent culture, it is most easy to get caught up in accumulating stuff: houses, cars, stocks, vacations, furniture, clothes, impressive friends, on and on. Even when we don't have the financial resources for all that we want, we can get caught up in coveting these things. Know this: Anyone who gives in to loving stuff will discover that the appetite never ends and the stuff accumulated will never satisfy, no matter how much is acquired. Most important, the pursuit of stuff will rob you of enjoying God's blessing and each other.

Lord, we face hundreds of choices every day. It's easy to get caught up in our world. Everything around us says that success is wealth, fame, and power. Help us to want to see Your perspective on life. Help us to seek ways to simplify our lives and to use our resources to further Your kingdom, not squander it on ourselves. All good things come from You, Lord, and we acknowledge You as our provider. Amen.

REFLECTION

"When we live in simplicity, we make a statement with our lives. We are saying that God is our provider. We see life and days and sunshine as gifts. We stop trying to control and manipulate. We stop fussing and positioning. We stop striving for what perishes. We become wise enough not to chase illusions. Most of all, we start hearing God's voice again. When this happens, the magic of happiness returns."

Bob Benson, *Disciplines for the Inner Life*

"A couple must find out for themselves where the various 'spheres of influence' lie: who pays the bills, who casts the deciding vote on buying what house, renting which apartment, where to vacation. A selfish husband or wife may insist on rendering a final verdict on all decisions, major and minor; but marriage involves resolving the incompatible needs of two different people."

Cecil Osborne, *The Art of Understanding Your Mate*

LET'S TALK ABOUT IT

1 How is the decision-making process done in your marriage now? What changes do you think need to take place?

2 How good are the two of you at controlling "impulse" decision making?

YOUR NOTES/REFLECTIONS/PRAYERS/GOALS

_____

_____

_____

_____

_____

_____

_____

_____

_____

_____

_____

Making Wise Choices

PURPOSE

FOR LIVING

25

Where there is no vision, the people perish.

Proverbs 29:18, KJV

PRAYER

Lord, thank You for creating both of us with certain gifts. Thank You, too, for bringing us together as a couple. We believe that You have called us together and have for us a purpose that will bring honor to Your name. May we prayerfully, continually seek Your purpose for our lives. May we fulfill the purpose You have for us as individuals, as a couple, and as a family. May we be faithful to give our best efforts and attention to the mission You have for us. In Jesus' name, amen.

SCRIPTURE

"And we know that God causes everything to work together for the good of those who love God and are called according to his purpose for them" (Rom. 8:28).

Having purpose is seeing the long-term reason for our lives as a couple. Purpose gives us a vision of the possibilities and helps us focus our intent to accomplish them.

When Nancie and I were first married, we already knew we had a shared purpose for living. We knew that we were called to help others grow spiritually while we grew ourselves. Our calling was to minister in ways that would strengthen others. In our thirty years of marriage, that calling has taken many twists and turns, from being teachers, youth pastors, pastors, publishers of family magazines, counselors, writers, and seminar speakers.

But all the time, we measured the twists and changes against the original purpose to help others grow spiritually and emotionally and to help families with their parenting and marriage skills. A shared purpose has helped us focus our lives in a direction that has a sense of continuity. When we started out, we did not know that someday we would publish magazines or write books; we just knew we wanted to use our gifts to build God's kingdom.

Your purpose may or may not be wrapped up in your vocation. Purpose speaks of a larger agenda than just your vocation. Purpose includes the goals you set for your marriage and family, the growth you set out to achieve spiritually, the effort you put into building the kingdom of God and in contrib-

uting to your community in ways that leave the world a better place.

Shared purpose means you and your spouse are headed in the same direction. You both want to achieve similar things in life. When two people share a vision of the way things ought to be and join together in the struggle to achieve that purpose, it is a powerful force. Great joy comes out of knowing your purpose for living. I often say that family life must be more than "us three and TV." By that I mean that the purpose you, your spouse, and your children have must extend beyond your own four walls. Your purpose must include reaching out to others. When you develop your purpose, you will find great joy in living.

Purpose also involves the spiritual dimension of our lives. In premarital counseling, I often ask couples how much time they have spent discussing their spiritual goals. Often they look at me in a puzzled way, as if that was an aspect of their relationship that would take care of itself. I tell them it is vital for them to think about their purpose for living. Marriage is not just having the wedding and going off to live in bliss with each other. Engaged couples and newlyweds must think about the spiritual dimension of their relationship and ask crucial questions: Who are we? Why are we here? How do we stay close to God and follow his calling for our lives? It is vital that we commit to pray with and for each other. It is imperative that we share a spiritual vision.

Purpose for Living

Think about your own life as a couple. You have talent and ability. You have a contribution to make to this life and to the kingdom of God. You have a marriage to craft. You may have children to raise, innovative ministries to start, books to write, songs to compose and sing, paintings to paint, lives of integrity and faith to live, people to mentor, and ten thousand more. These take vision and struggle and staying on the path.

How do we realize our purpose and fulfill the vision God has for us? First, we learn to trust God and believe that He really does have a plan for our lives and that we are capable of accomplishing our purpose if we will trust God to empower us on a day-by-day basis. Second, we set specific goals in all areas of our lives, which is what we ask you to pray for in the next chapter.

Lord, sometimes we feel imprisoned by what seems to be the urgent instead of looking at the big picture. Help us dream big dreams with You, Lord, and not settle for second best. Help us move from the quest for success to the quest for significance. Help us to find our calling as a couple and to stand before you on that final day and hear you say, "Well done, good and faithful servants." In Christ's name, amen.

REFLECTION

"We have come to suspect strongly that dreams—expectations—shared, talked about, discussed, are some of the ingredients from which durable and lasting marriages are made."

Floyd and Harriet Thatcher, *Long-Term Marriage*

"We are called to cultivate Christ in our spouses by the power of the spoken word. To do so effectively, we must be guided by a vision of who they are, a picture of who they were meant to be (like Christ), and a grasp of our role in helping them become like Christ."

Dan B. Allender and Tremper Longman III, *Intimate Allies*

LET'S TALK ABOUT IT

1 Try writing a mission statement for your marriage relationship. This will help you identify your calling and purpose.

2 List the individual gifts that God has given each of you and discuss how they contribute to your calling and mission. How can the two of you enhance your purpose together?

YOUR NOTES/REFLECTIONS/PRAYERS/GOALS

Purpose for Living

PRAYING FOR THE PRESENCE OF GOD IN OUR

GOALS

26

Forgetting what is behind and straining toward what is ahead, I press on toward the

goal to win the prize for which God has called me heavenward in Christ Jesus.

Philippians 3:13-14, NIV

PRAYER

Lord, help us to order our day-to-day agendas so that we build a life of principle and purpose as you have planned for us. Help us to develop habits and goals that produce Christlikeness in our marriage. Give us eyes to see the important things, to plan for noble things for our life together. Give us wisdom to be good stewards of the time and resources You give us. May we plan to build into Your kingdom, to invest wisely. Help us daily to invest the best in our marriage. Amen.

SCRIPTURE

"Run in such a way as to get the prize" (1 Cor. 9:24, NIV).

Duncan and Cindy Campbell are a couple I (Bill) admire very much. Early on, Duncan set out to get a good education. He is both a licensed attorney and a certified public accountant. He and Cindy work side by side in many ways. They have set goals for their lives and have accomplished a great deal in their business as well as in building the kingdom of God. The Campbells decided to use a substantial portion of their wealth to start a ministry, which they named Friends of the Children. This kingdom-building organization has several full-time professionals who act as mentors for inner-city children who might otherwise grow up in a life of crime and abuse. With the consent of the children's parents, the mentors befriend the children, help them with their schoolwork, take them on outings, and do whatever it takes to build the children's self-esteem and to show them a better world.

It was just six years ago that the Campbells planted the seed money to start this outreach. The staff now includes thirty full-time, paid mentors who are each assigned eight young children. This accomplishment is all the more amazing because both Duncan and Cindy came from dysfunctional homes. Duncan's parents were alcoholics who basically abandoned him as a child. They both died before Duncan finished college. Duncan said, "From the time I was a child, my goal was to make

something of my life and not end up like my parents."

I recently asked Duncan and Cindy how they had accomplished their vision to begin a ministry. Duncan said, "In whatever we do, we always start out by asking God what He wants. When we think we sense God's heart on something, we write down the broad goal or objective and the desired outcome. We then go back and break it down to several small goals that are achievable. We strongly believe in measuring results."

While you and your spouse may not have the resources to do what the Campbells have done, you can accomplish a great deal if you will set daily, weekly, monthly, and yearly goals. Having a purpose for living is having vision (which is what you were praying for in the last chapter). However, in order to fulfill our vision and purpose, we must set goals. Having goals means having a plan of action. Goals are measurable steps to fulfilling our dream and God's calling for our lives. Goals give us direction and a target.

Your goals should include spiritual goals, ministry goals, family goals, educational goals, occupational goals, financial goals, personal goals, and marriage goals. Long-term goals should be broken into several smaller (milestone or short-term) goals.

For example, last year Nancie set a goal to read the entire Bible through in one year. She

Goals

accomplished that by setting a daily reading schedule. This year I have set a goal to do the same. I bought a One Year Bible that already has the daily reading schedule mapped out.

As a couple you might set a goal to pray together for at least five or ten minutes every day. If you're both very busy, you might set a goal to eat a relaxing meal together at least once every day so that you can take the time for each of you to converse, listen, and be heard. As a family, you might set a goal to save enough money over the next two years to take a missions trip to a third-world country. If you are going to help your children with their college education, you will need to set a goal to contribute to a college fund on a regular basis.

Nancie and I recently decided to set a goal to simplify our lifestyle. It is one thing to say this is what we want to do; it is quite another to set up a step-by-step plan to accomplish it. Our goal over the next few years includes these steps: getting out of nearly all debt; if and when we need another vehicle, to buy a used car rather than a new one; to limit credit-card spending to business travel only; to give more of our resources to God's work; to eventually move to a smaller house now that our kids are almost all out of the nest; to do less dining out; to contribute a certain amount to our savings account every month; and to avoid buying anything on impulse.

By setting noble and achievable goals, we order our lives into a plan of action. When we look back, we can see that little by little, day by day, goal by goal, we have accomplished a great deal. God is pleased when we plan our lives in ways that help us accomplish His purpose for us.

Lord, help us to set daily goals that lead us toward the purpose You have for us. Help us to discipline our lives so that what we do counts for eternity. Help us to measure our days and give priority for spiritual growth. Show us Your plan for our lives and then help us to set the goals that achieve good things for You. Amen.

REFLECTION

"Your own wishes and dreams must coincide with your mate's and be within the realm of attainment for you—neither beneath nor beyond you. For if they are not realistically built and mutually carried out, they lead to frustration and stagnation in marriage rather than to emotional comfort."

David Abrahamsen, quoted in *Long-Term Marriage*

"Married life . . . isn't a time for settling down but for growth, for doing new things. With each passing year a growing couple will actively look for new and different things they can do together."

Dale Evans Rogers, "God in the Hard Times"

LET'S TALK ABOUT IT

1 Write down on paper where you would like to be in five years and ten years—spiritually, educationally, occupationally, financially, and in your marriage and family. Break down these dreams or goals into one-year goals. Then set some short-term goals (monthly, weekly, daily) you can start now in order to accomplish the long-term goals.

2 Pray together and commit this plan to the Lord and ask Him to help you be faithful in the daily process of accomplishing this plan.

YOUR NOTES/REFLECTIONS/PRAYERS/GOALS

_____

_____

_____

_____

_____

_____

_____

_____

_____

_____

_____

Goals

HANDLING
MONEY

27

. . . .

Now, a person who is put in charge as a manager must be faithful.

1 Corinthians 4:2

PRAYER

Lord, we want to be good stewards with our finances. We recognize You as our source, and we know that You have a plan that includes how we use our financial resources. Give us Your wisdom and a willingness to obey You. Help us to invest wisely, to save prudently, and to give hilariously. In Jesus' name, amen.

SCRIPTURE

"And why worry about your clothes? Look at the lilies and how they grow. They don't work or make their clothing, yet Solomon in all his glory was not dressed as beautifully as they are. And if God cares so wonderfully for flowers that are here today and gone tomorrow, won't he more surely care for you? . . . So don't worry about having enough. . . . Why be like the pagans who are so deeply concerned about these things?" (Matt. 6:28-32).

One of the major stress points in marriages today is the issue of finances. In our culture, we tend to get sucked into a consumer lifestyle that always wants more.

In trying to live the American dream, it's easy to get trapped by consumption that produces debt, which, in turn, produces stress. Arguing over spending and budgets is a major problem that erodes marriages in our culture. Of the many couples I have seen for marriage counseling, I would estimate that more than half of these couples point to disagreements over financial issues as a part of their problem. And even in the other half, finances often play an indirect role because both husband and wife are working full-time outside the home in order to keep up. This puts stress on raising a family, spending time together, sharing the workload, and many other aspects of marriage.

I asked my friend Pat Clements, president of Church Extension Plan (a financial resource institution for churches and laypersons), how he would advise a Christian couple to be free of financial stress. "Financial bondage," he said, "is caused not by lack of money but by lack of contentment. Scripture challenges us to seek an attitude of contentment whether we are financially abundant or suffer financial need. Paul tells us in Philippians 4:12, 'I know how to live on almost nothing or with everything. I have learned the secret of living

in every situation, whether it is with a full stomach or empty, with plenty or little. For I can do everything with the help of Christ who gives me the strength I need.'"

Pat teaches couples that financial freedom involves the following:

- Freedom from debt—from owing more than we have in cash or assets.
- Freedom from financial pressure—from the fear of unexpected expenses because every dollar is budgeted to meet obligations.
- Freedom from loving money—from focusing on the goal of getting rich.
- Freedom from entanglement—from allowing business and investment cares to crowd out our love for God.
- Freedom from get-rich-quick schemes—from looking for ways to make large amounts of money without the investment of labor or effort.
- Freedom from financial guilt or bitterness—from using others (or being used by others) for financial gain and from accusations over real or imagined unfairness in past business transactions.

Married couples need to remember that God provides us with clear financial principles. Jesus had as much to say about money as He did about anything else. God associates our ability to handle spiritual matters with our ability to handle financial matters. Jesus said,

"If you are untrustworthy about worldly wealth, who will trust you with the true riches of heaven?" (Luke 16:11).

Nancie and I have learned that the Lord often uses our finances to confirm direction. We have discovered that God is able to provide funds for specific things as an indication of His will and to withhold funds as an indication of a different direction He may want us to go. When we started publishing *Virtue* magazine, we believed it was God's will for us, but we did not have the financial backing. We prayed, "Lord, if this is your will, we need You to confirm this by providing the resources we need." Rather than just sitting back and waiting, we began exploring avenues of opportunity. Local banks laughed at us when we approached them for a loan to start a Christian publishing company. But God led us to a Christian bank president who loaned us enough money to get started. Through many financial miracles, we saw God's hand of provision to continue publishing the magazine. Some weeks we thought we would not have enough money to meet payroll, but by the end of the week the money was there to meet our

obligations. We never missed a payroll, and we always were able to pay our bills on time. Each week became a powerful confirmation that what we were doing was God's will for our lives. This experience taught us about how God wants to be our source and how He will make a way for His will to be accomplished through us.

In many of the marriage surveys that we did, couples consistently told us that some of the most bonding and exciting projects they did together were business or ministry ventures. Yes, there was potential for stress and failure, but the couples repeatedly shared how they had been stretched and how they had grown together by having to trust God for things beyond their reach.

Lord, keep us from getting trapped into buying bigger houses, better cars, more stuff, with more debt. Help us to see that You want us to be free from the burden of financial stress, and give us wisdom to make good choices with our resources. Give us the courage to let You lead us by letting You be our provider. Help us to trust You rather than material things. In Jesus' name, amen.

REFLECTION

"To get money is difficult, to keep it more difficult, but to spend it wisely, most difficult of all."

Unknown

"I spoke with a friend who is a successful businessman and an elder in his congregation. Over the years he has counseled more than fifty couples who were in deep financial difficulty. When they came to him for advice about solving their money problems, he agreed to help if they would decide to give ten cents of every dollar they made to the Lord. My friend said every couple who followed through not only got their financial house in order, they had the opportunity to do good for God. That's a tremendous track record!"

Kregg Hood, *Take God at His Word*

LET'S TALK ABOUT IT

1 Together discuss your financial priorities. If you are not already tithing regularly, start now. If you need to simplify, write down your current budget and look for places to cut. If you have more money than you need, ask God how you can use your money to build His kingdom.

2 If you are in debt, visit a financial counseling center (usually free) that will help you restructure your debt load and help you begin the climb toward financial freedom.

Handling Money

YOUR NOTES/REFLECTIONS/PRAYERS/GOALS

_____

_____

_____

_____

_____

_____

_____

I set before you today life and prosperity, death and destruction. For I command you today to love the Lord your God, to walk in his ways. . . . Now choose life, so that you and your children may live and . . . hold fast to him. For the Lord is your life.

Deuteronomy 30:15-16,19-20, NIV

PRAYER

Lord, time is a precious gift, yet how easy it is to squander it. Too often we fill our minds with banal things that have no lasting value to us individually, to us as a couple, or to Your kingdom. Give us discernment, Lord, to order our days so that we may redeem the time You have given us. Help us as a couple to build for eternity. Amen.

SCRIPTURE

"Be careful how you live, not as fools but as those who are wise. Make the most of every opportunity for doing good in these evil days" (Eph. 5:15-16).

When Bill and I were first married, we had a lot of conflict over our day off. Would we do what he wanted or what I wanted? For some reason, we don't have that argument anymore—maybe because it's rare to have a day off, or maybe because we've grown to want to do the same things! But we've come to realize that time is our most valuable resource.

It is easy in our opportunity-rich world to be overwhelmed and disorganized with our time, and often we end up pressured by commitments we neither wanted nor planned. In her book *Stress and the Healthy Family,* Delores Curran reports that one of the leading stressors in a family is not having enough time. The majority of married couples reported that they had "insufficient couple time" and "insufficient 'me' time." Many couples in our survey reported that when their schedules got too full, two essential things got crowded out: time together as a couple and time with God. Is that true of your marriage? Let's look at a few things that may help you protect your time.

How do you spend your time? We spend our lives, minute by minute, hour by hour, working, commuting, watching television, talking on the telephone, eating, going to our kids' activities, and shopping. We would hope that we also spend time praying, going to church, reading God's Word, reaching out to those in need, and listening to the needs of

those we love. What are the activities and commitments that consume your time?

How do you want to spend your time? How we spend our time and how we *want* to spend our time are two different issues. The challenge is to gain control over our time so that we can spend it wisely, on things that matter to us. Some couples have found that when they answered these two questions, they discovered that they were frittering away their time in things that didn't matter or that didn't enhance their relationship. They realized that watching TV was their greatest time waster.

Schedule time to be together. Don't leave spending time together as a couple to chance. Just as we write appointments into our calendars for the doctor and for work-related meetings, we need to do that for our couple time as well.

Use the time you do have together wisely. When we examine our schedules, we often discover that we do have time together, but we don't use it very well. Sometimes we are in the same room with our spouse for hours at a time, but we are preoccupied with the newspaper or some other distraction. It is as if we were living those moments on different continents! Be careful that the precious time you do have together as a daily part of life does not just evaporate because of some other preoccupation.

Learn the art of saying no. Many of us say yes too often to too many requests and/or demands.

Managing Time

Our boss wants us to work overtime; the youth pastor wants us to help on a weekend outing; our friends want us to play golf with them (for the third time this week); the service club wants us to volunteer to help out at the fair booth; the school wants us to help out on a field trip; our broker wants us to attend a special investment opportunity meeting. On and on it goes. These are all good things, in their time. But if they crowd out "couple" time and "God" time, they are robbing us of the essentials. When this happens, we need to say no to some good opportunities so that we can say yes to even better choices: our marriage and our relationship to the Lord.

Just this week, Bill and I were feeling under pressure with the deadline for finishing this book, and time seemed urgent, in short supply. It was time for our church's midweek prayer service, and we didn't have time to go. Yet somehow we sensed an urgency to be there, to worship with each other and with other believers. Was it a coincidence that our pastor spoke about time? I don't think so. We came away renewed and refreshed, both individually and as a couple. Our time is in God's hands, and when we worship Him by being good stewards of our time, we find that somehow the work does get done and life together as a couple and with God is put in its proper place as well.

Lord, thank You for giving us this day. So many times we are preoccupied by what is going to happen next week or next month that we fail to see the wonderful day that You have given us. May we have the courage and discipline to talk to one another about how we fill our days. Give us thoughtfulness and originality. Amen.

REFLECTION

"We are not infinite. The day does not have more than twenty-four hours. We do not have an inexhaustible source of human energy. . . . Overloading is the enemy. Some will respond: 'I can do all things through Christ who strengthens me.' Can you? Can you fly? Can you go six months without eating? Neither can you live a healthy life chronically overloaded. . . . Jesus did not heal all, He did not minister to all, He did not visit all, and He did not teach all. . . . It is God the Creator who made limits, and it is the same God who placed them within us for our protection. We exceed them at our peril."

Richard A. Swenson, *Margin*

"TV itself, that noisy box in the corner of the living room, has become an equal—an essential—partner in many marriages. Even when it's turned off, there's that blank screen waiting to rejoin the conversation or to monopolize one's time or worse, one's spouse's attentions."

David Hellerstein, "Can TV Cause Divorce?"

LET'S TALK ABOUT IT

1. Make dates to be together. Use some of this time to coordinate your calendars so that you can make wise choices about how you spend your time. Once a year take an extended time—an overnight trip, if possible—to discuss your goals and dreams and to decide how you will make time to realize these goals and dreams.

2. Agree to keep TV watching to a minimum. Write down the programs you want to watch, then hold yourselves accountable to the list.

YOUR NOTES/REFLECTIONS/PRAYERS/GOALS

_____

_____

_____

_____

_____

_____

_____

_____

_____

_____

_____

SHARING WORK

29

All the believers were of one heart and mind, and they felt that what they owned

was not their own; they shared everything they had.

Acts 4:32

PRAYER

Lord, help us to be completely fair to each other in how we handle the duties and chores of our lives. Help us to be a team, giving the help when and where needed. Help us to be sensitive to each other's workload. Help us to find the balance that avoids any resentment or sense of injustice. In Jesus' name, amen.

SCRIPTURE

"I ask you, my true teammate, to help these women, for they worked hard with me in telling others the Good News. . . . Always be full of joy in the Lord. I say it again—rejoice! Let everyone see that you are considerate in all you do. Remember, the Lord is coming soon" (Phil. 4:3-5).

Let me tell you right up front that this chapter is written to convict me (Bill) and all husbands like me. I confess that Nancie does more than her share of the work in our house. In addition to having a heavy speaking and writing ministry, she faithfully maintains the house for the rest of us. We all chip in some, but she is the main one, and frankly I do not know what we would do without her. Certainly, we would not have clean clothes, a clean house, or warm meals very often. I am grateful but guilt ridden!

I do some things, like clean the garage (twice a year) and mow the yard in the summer (also about twice a year). I pay the bills and keep our finances straight. Oh yeah, I also shake the rugs when she is cleaning the house, and I try to do the dishes once in a while. I will also go grocery shopping when she asks me to, which she doesn't very often because I end up bringing home things she didn't put on her list, like ice cream and chips. When our kids were younger, I fixed breakfast nearly every morning for our children before they left for school. Any repairs needed around the house, I take care of too (I call the plumber or heating man). And probably the biggest chore I do for Nancie involves two things she absolutely hates: I dispose of mice when they get in our traps around the house, and I kill spiders. Nancie believes that these two reasons alone make it worth keeping me around, so I am a lucky man indeed! I am not

proud of my personal track record regarding this. (Maybe this is why Nancie insisted I write this chapter!)

With more and more women working outside the home these days, it is very important that we take some inventory about who is doing what around the house. Several studies show that even where one might expect a more equal division of labor, housework is relatively optional for men. Women who work outside the home still spend more than twice as many hours on housework and chores around the house as do their husbands.

We husbands clearly need to improve. We give our wives lame excuses such as, "I don't mind sharing the housework, but I don't do it very well. We should each do things we're best at." Which really means, "Unfortunately I'm not good at things like cooking or washing dishes. What I do best is a little light carpentry, changing light bulbs, or moving furniture (which is done about once a year)." It might also mean or at least be interpreted by our wives as meaning, "I don't like the dull, stupid, boring jobs, so you should do them."

Another common excuse men use is, "We have different standards. Why does everything need to be so squeaky clean?" Which really means, "I know I can wait longer than you as dirt and filth pile up in this house. I also know that all women have a syndrome called 'guilt over a messy house,' and if I wait long enough you will clean up this mess."

Here are some suggestions at coming to a more amicable solution:

Husbands, shape up! Some husbands are the exception, but most of us need to prayerfully consider the inequities in what happens around our house and ask God to help us be more fair about dividing up the chores-at-home pie. We husbands need to realize that when we don't do our fair share, it is no laughing matter for our wives. It is also unfair.

Wives, consider a new approach. One woman said her problem was solved when she and her husband started a system: "Rather than keeping track of who does what job, we keep an eye on how much free time we each get. We focus on making sure we each get a fair share of free time. No job (paid or unpaid) has any more value than another in our house. Some may have higher priority, but if I wash dishes while he earns the money, we have both given up time. Since we have gone to this system, we don't fight anymore about it. Perhaps because now we both respect and value each other so much that we want to do all we can to make our life together easier for each other."

Another wife told us, "I suggest options to my husband. For instance, I say, 'Would you rather feed the baby or get her bottles ready?' or 'Would you rather do the dishes or give the baby a bath?' He can't really say 'neither.' (Well, he could, but he'd be in big trouble if he did!)"

Another wife said she has taken a new view of things. "I used to get upset if my husband didn't do what I asked immediately. Now, if he says he'll do the dishes but doesn't jump right up and do them, I don't get upset. I know he'll do them, but he'll do them in his way and on his timetable. I've learned to be satisfied with that."

Lord, forgive us for being selfish at times. Forgive us for our lack of consideration when we do not sense the needs of our spouse. Help us to be quick to find ways to help each other with the duties and responsibilities we face. Help each of us to be quick to take responsibility to do our fair share of the work around our house. We know, Lord, that it pleases You when we go the extra mile to help each other, and we want to please You. In Christ's name, amen.

Sharing Work

REFLECTION

"The way you team up with each other reflects the way you love each other. It shows how sensitive you are to each other's needs and problems. Teamwork is love, and love is teamwork. In marriage they are inseparable and mutually dependent."

V. Gilbert and Arlisle Beers, quoted in *Husbands and Wives*

"There is no 'right' or 'wrong' way for a particular family to divide housework. The interests, abilities, traditions, and other obligations of each family member play a part in determining how much housework a family performs and who does it. Ideally, a family creates a division of labor based upon the needs and talents of each family member as well as the best of tradition."

Gary L. Hanson and Mary Buchanan Moore, "Work and Family Challenges"

LET'S TALK ABOUT IT

1 Add points for the chores you and your spouse perform. If you share a chore, split the point value: taking kids to soccer (or other) practice (2); changing sheets (3); gardening (3); minor household repairs (3); vacuuming (3); buying birthday/Christmas presents (4); changing diapers (4); cooking dinner (4); doing laundry (4); dusting (4); grocery shopping (4); taking out garbage (4); washing car (4); cleaning sinks and tubs (5); mopping floors (5); mowing yard (5); washing dishes (5); washing pet (5); dealing with repair people (6); paying bills (6); cleaning out fridge (6); ironing (7); cleaning toilets (8); cleaning oven (8); cleaning garage (8).

2 If the points are fairly even, the work is too. If not, discuss ways to bring it into balance.

Sharing Work

YOUR NOTES/REFLECTIONS/PRAYERS/GOALS

_____

_____

_____

_____

_____

_____

_____

PART 6

Respect

Acceptance

Nondefensiveness

Honesty

Tenderness

Loyalty

Trust

RESEPCT

30

Show respect for everyone. Love your Christian brothers and sisters.

1 Peter 2:17

PRAYER

Lord, we learn from Your Word that showing respect is a powerful way to show love. When we show respect for our spouse, we are recognizing the fact that he or she is a unique being created in Your image—a precious person for whom You died. We pray that we will learn how to offer respect to each other. Amen.

SCRIPTURE

"Evil words destroy one's friends; wise discernment rescues the godly" (Prov. 11:9).

Something amazing happens when we offer respect to people, even if they don't immediately seem to deserve it. They tend to become better people, to somehow try to live up to that respect. Josi and Brad were having extreme difficulties in their marriage of twenty years. They told us, "We are very different from each other, and both of us are impatient with each other's differences. We had been to counseling, and although we learned new insights, nothing seemed to change." A turning point came when Josi said God spoke to her and said she needed to change her attitude toward her marriage and respect her husband. She did, and a dramatic change happened between them. She confided, "That brought about an atmosphere that allowed him to grow into the man God wanted him to be, and God is continuing to mold us into His image."

Respect means treating one another with dignity, valuing the other's opinions, intelligence, and judgment. When we offer respect to someone, we are affirming that person's worth. God values our individual personalities and gifts, and He values us just for who we are. We must offer the same respect to others. We can lose sight of what respect means when we do not appreciate the very real differences that we have.

Respect is also an issue of equality. As one traditional wedding ceremony reminds us, "If the man is the head, she is the crown—

a crown to her husband. The man was dust refined, but the woman was doubly refined—one step further from the earth. In being created from man, or out of man, she was not out of his head to dominate, or to be over him; nor out of his feet to be under him, or trampled upon by him; but out of his side to be equal with him, from under his arm to be protected by him, and near to his heart to be loved." Respect gives a sense of being on equal footing with one another.

Craig told us he had a difficult time respecting his wife. She wasn't living up to what he thought was her potential, and she seemed to make no effort to try. We encouraged him to respect her for what she *was:* the mother of his children and the woman whom he had vowed, before God and family, to love. We encouraged him to verbalize his respect in these two areas. Over a period of several months, Craig discovered that as he showed respect for his wife in these areas, his disrespect in other areas lessened.

How do we actually show respect? We can show respect by how we speak to each other. One of the rules we have tried to keep in our house is never to speak in diminishing ways to each other. We have tried to teach our children this rule as well. It is fine to disagree. It is acceptable to confront. But it is never acceptable to use cutting words to attack another family member's character or person. We also show our respect by what we say about our spouse to our children or others. When a husband hears his wife say to their children, "Your dad is such a thoughtful person. He returned your library books for you when he realized they were overdue," his self-image grows.

It seems that men and women receive respect differently. A woman feels respected if she feels heard, not told what to do. A man feels respected if he is trusted, not given unasked-for advice. Our personal honor and self-esteem are preserved in an atmosphere of respect, and we have the privilege and trust to deepen that respect. Our ability to communicate with each other is enhanced through mutual respect. In fact, everything in our marriage from our sex life to our personal growth will flourish as the result of mutual respect.

What if your spouse does not respect you? First of all, you must respect yourself as God's creation. Others tend to respond to you the way you see yourself. Sue learned a painful lesson about this. She said for several years she tried to do things that she thought her husband and his family expected of her, even though it was not "her." She said when she finally learned to respect herself and her own God-given gifts, she gained the respect of her husband and family as well. Second, if you feel your spouse doesn't respect you, try to talk about it, giving your spouse examples: "I felt disrespect from you when I heard you talk to Jack about my disagreement with Cheri" or "I feel as if you don't respect me when you joke about me when we're with my family."

Lord, how important is this quality of respect. It is, ultimately, acknowledging Your creation. Give us the grace to offer respect for one another as a way of showing our respect for You. In Christ's name, amen.

REFLECTION

"More romance in your marriage may depend on your choice to accept and treasure your husband for who he is. If he doesn't sense acceptance and feels you're pushing him to change, he may become more resistant. Your husband needs to feel love unconditionally."

Jean Lush, quoted in *Today's Christian Woman*

"The quality of our character is most revealed in little things, not big things. Christianity finds its truest test in traffic, when the car breaks down, when an appointment suddenly cancels at the last moment, and in the confines of marriage. . . . How we are behind the tightly drawn curtains of our own private castle is how we really are. . . . Show some respect."

Patrick Morley, *Two-Part Harmony*

1 This may take some courage, but as lovingly and honestly as possible, tell your spouse what actions or words make you feel disrespected.

2 Ask your spouse, "What actions or words of mine help you feel respected?" Then consciously try to demonstrate respect to your spouse, and watch the results!

YOUR NOTES/REFLECTIONS/PRAYERS/GOALS

_____

_____

_____

_____

_____

_____

_____

_____

_____

_____

_____

_____

_____

Respect

PRAYING FOR THE PRESENCE OF GOD IN OUR

ACCEPTANCE

31

Stop judging others, and you will not be judged. . . . Do for others what

you would like them to do for you.

Matthew 7:1, 12

PRAYER

Lord, You know how different we are from each other, and the longer we live together, the more our differences seem apparent. It seems we can see our spouse's faults and weaknesses better than we see our own. Give each of us a fresh understanding of our very real differences, and help us not to attack these differences, but rather protect and defend each other from the vulnerability that comes from these areas. Help both of us, Lord, to accept each other. In Jesus' name, amen.

SCRIPTURE

"Disregarding another person's faults preserves love; telling about them separates close friends"
(Prov. 17:9).

As husbands and wives we are one, but we are also very different from each other. God created each of us unique, and we come into the marriage with different ways of looking at life. That can either be a source of frustration or growth. When we understand and accept each other's differences rather than fight them, we place ourselves in a good position to grow from and be able to celebrate those differences.

In one of our earlier books, *That Man! Understanding the Differences Between You and Your Husband,* Nancie and I discussed the biological, social, emotional, and spiritual differences between men and women. Men and women view life through different lenses. Men tend to be more analytical and abstract in problem solving; women tend to maintain a relational identity with the problem. Men are taught that emotions can be a sign of weakness; women are taught that it's important to express emotions. Men are taught to be tough; women are taught to be tender. Men tend to use one side of their brain to solve spatial problems, the other side to verbalize; women tend to use both sides of their brain at once. Men have more testosterone; women have more estrogen. I could go on and on pointing out the differences.

In his book *Bonding: Relationships in the Image of God,* Donald Joy relates many of the male-female differences to the Fall in the Garden of Eden. He says that two basic things

happened at the time of original sin. First, the world went haywire and ceased to be a perfect place; and second, a pure relationship with God was disrupted and broken. He goes on to say that males are task oriented, preoccupied with trying to fix what went wrong with the universe, while women are relationship oriented, preoccupied with trying to restore the disrupted relationship.

The bottom line is that we are different. As Nancie and I said in our book, "Unfortunately, our egalitarian society has confused equality with sameness. In the name of equal opportunity we have tried to obliterate the differences between sexes and cultures. In doing so, we have lost sight of the uniqueness of each."

Nancie and I spent a lot of years in our marriage trying to fix each other. Here's what we've learned: it doesn't work. Instead it tends to erode the relationship. The fact remains that we are two very imperfect people with plenty of faults to go around. For some reason, it's always easier to see someone else's faults and think we can fix him or her. Nancie wanted me to be more spontaneous, less uptight about things; I wanted her to be more organized. We're thankful that over the years we have come to appreciate the differences in each other, and we've both actually been able to change in some ways. But until we felt accepted and appreciated for who and

Acceptance

what we were, we found it nearly impossible to change.

We can be very threatened by differences. *Different* does not mean we are defective. It merely means we are different. Our differences will crop up in a thousand ways: the foods we like; the TV programs we prefer to watch; the emotions we experience in the same situation; the ideas we have about sex, disciplining kids, spending money, showing affection, solving problems, and on and on. Differences are a fact of life. Instead of fighting them, we need to celebrate them yet be sensitive to each other and maintain an attitude of compromise and conciliation.

Instead of fretting over these differences, we need to accept them, celebrate them, and learn to enjoy them. One of you might be better with handling financial matters, while the other has an eye for interior decorating. You may be good at cooking up wonderful recipes while your spouse can fix almost anything. A husband might be more outgoing, but the wife might be more insightful. He might pray in a stoic manner; she might weep when she prays. Basically, if you look closely enough, you will probably find that you compensate for and complement one another with your strengths.

Lord, teach us to accept each other's differences. Help us to celebrate the unique way You have created us, realizing that You put us together to complete us. Help us to accept our spouse's strengths and weaknesses. And help us to practice seeing life from our spouse's point of view and to respect that point of view as being an equal part of the relationship. Amen.

Acceptance

R E F L E C T I O N

"Human love constructs its own image of the other person, of what he is and what he should become. It takes the life of the other person into its own hands. Spiritual love recognizes the true image of the other person which he has received from Jesus Christ; the image that Jesus Christ Himself embodied and would stamp on all of me."

Dietrich Bonhoeffer, *Life Together*

"The way to love someone is to lightly run your finger over the person's soul until you find a crack, and then gently pour your love into that crack."

Keith Miller, quoted in *Quiet Moments for Couples*

1 What differences are causing conflicts in your marriage? What can you do to accept and embrace those differences?

2 What unique qualities do you and your spouse bring to your marriage? How do these qualities complement your relationship and make you stronger?

YOUR NOTES/REFLECTIONS/PRAYERS/GOALS

Acceptance

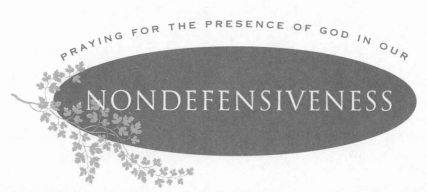

NONDEFENSIVENESS

32 . . . .

You must clothe yourselves with tenderhearted mercy, kindness, humility,

gentleness, and patience. You must make allowance for each other's faults and

forgive the person who offends you. . . . The most important piece

of clothing you must wear is love.

Colossians 3:12-14

PRAYER

Lord, I find that I do a lot of manipulating to get my own way. Sometimes I have a hard time seeing someone else's point of view, especially my spouse's. Give me the skill to negotiate and the willingness to be nondefensive. Help me not to play the "blame game" but to accept responsibility for myself. Help me to listen to my spouse before I speak. Help me to get in the habit of saying, "Maybe you're right." Amen.

"But the wisdom that comes from heaven is first of all pure. It is also . . . willing to yield to others. It is full of mercy and good deeds. It shows no partiality and is always sincere" (James 3:17).

INSIGHT

Tom and Patty have been married almost eight years and have two small children. They both know something is very wrong with their relationship, but they aren't sure what. They are committed to one another, yet they are often verbally at each other's throats over petty things. They are quick to point a finger at the other and are slow to take responsibility for their own actions.

Tom realized that something had to be done because their attitudes toward one another were eroding their love. After prayer and counsel, without determining who was "right" or "wrong," they both agreed simply to call a truce, to put down their defensiveness. It was amazing what happened between them as their marriage took on a new atmosphere.

I get defensive when I think someone is out to get me or will attack me, and I feel I have to protect myself and what belongs to me. Maybe you feel that way sometimes too.

We may become defensive in our marriage relationship for good reason. Perhaps we have gotten into a bad pattern of talking down to one another, or we have trampled on each other's boundaries. If that is the case, feelings

of resentment easily rise to the surface. Or being defensive with each other can just become a bad habit and part of the way we communicate. We may have grown up with certain attitudes that shape the way we view others. Being defensive in a marriage adds distance and drives a wedge between us. Being nondefensive breaks down barriers and makes us more appealing to one another.

Sometimes we need to stop and examine our attitudes. Bad attitudes can be contagious. We may be spending time with another couple who are defensive toward each other, and before we know it, we're bickering back and forth, too. We may be with others who do a lot of male bashing or female bashing, and we can start to see our spouse as an enemy, or at the very least, a spoiler of all our fun!

Being nondefensive in a relationship means choosing not to point fingers. When we are nondefensive, we do not have to prove we're right. We are approachable and vulnerable, not thin-skinned or touchy.

There is a secret strength in vulnerability. In his book *Intimacy,* Henri Nouwen wrote, "The encounter in love is an encounter with-

Nondefensiveness

out weapons. . . . We are very able to hide our guns and knives even in the most intimate relationship. An old bitter memory, a slight suspicion about motives or a small doubt can be as sharp as a knife held behind our back as a weapon for defense in case of attack."

When we are defensive, we blame others. In his book *The Fragile Bond*, Augustus Napier wrote, "Blaming is the scourge of marriage. We all do it, and it's always damaging and unproductive. While the diagnostic cue is the overuse of the word 'You'; 'You always forget our anniversary,' or 'You are just like your mother,' or 'You never clean up that mess,' much more is at stake than the overuse of 'You.' Since we have transferred our dependency on our parents to our mate, our blaming is really a product of this dependency. So the essence of blaming is the denial of responsibility for the self. Watch your

expectations in marriage. . . . Don't ask for help with your sense of self-worth, don't ask your partner to solve any of life's fundamental agonies. . . . If we can make this transition, we can achieve deeper intimacy than if we pretend the other is a parent to us."

Having a nondefensive attitude causes us to listen to one another with our hearts—to listen with a sense of caring, compassion, and vulnerability. Yet within that vulnerability, real love grows stronger.

Lord, how quick I am to protect myself, my turf. Teach me that true love means to put down my weapons of words and attitudes. Teach me to respond, not react. May I have the strength to be weak, knowing that You bless those who strive for peace. May my marriage be a mirror of Your strong love that goes on reaching even in rejection and mistakes. Amen.

Nondefensiveness

REFLECTION

"Three guidelines to communication in the early days of your marriage:
(1) Talk more freely about your feelings, but not in such a way that your partner
feels rebuked or criticized; (2) Be willing to show your vulnerable side to your mate.
A cardinal rule of developing intimacy is: Dare to be needy; do not be afraid to say, "I need you";
and (3) Remember that silence is almost always a negative feedback unless it is accompanied
by nonverbal signals that your partner shares your feelings,
such as by a squeeze of the hand or a smile."

Ed Wheat, *Love Life for Every Married Couple*

"In marriage it's important to remember, first of all, that we are all human beings and fallible. We have to give each other the space to be human, to have certain qualities that you do appreciate and other qualities that might not be so great. We're not always perfect or meet each other's standards."

Gwen Knights, quoted in *The Heart of Marriage*

LET'S TALK ABOUT IT

1. Is the attitude that you and your spouse have toward one another characterized more often by defensiveness or nondefensiveness?

2. If the blame game is part of your communication, discuss ways you can deal with it. Practice a new way to communicate truthfully and lovingly without using *you* words.

YOUR NOTES/REFLECTIONS/PRAYERS/GOALS

_____

_____

_____

_____

_____

_____

_____

_____

_____

_____

PRAYING FOR THE PRESENCE OF GOD IN OUR

HONESTY

33

But you desire honesty from the heart, so you can teach me

to be wise in my inmost being.

Psalm 51:6

PRAYER

Lord, we pray that You will help us to be truthful in our dealings with one another. Keep us from telling "little white lies" in an attempt to protect ourselves. May we make a habit of honesty. Even more, Lord, help us to realize that being truthful means more than just telling the truth. We pray that our intent would be absolute integrity with each other in heart, word, and deed. We pray for courage to be as transparent as humanly possible. In Christ's name, amen.

SCRIPTURE

"The Lord is more pleased when we do what is just and right than when we give him sacrifices"
(Prov. 21:3).

Honesty is a difficult concept to discuss because it seems obvious. Of course we are to be honest. Of course it's important. But honesty is challenging because it takes us to the core of who we are. And within a marriage, if we are completely honest at all times about our feelings and emotions, we could harm the marriage relationship. But honesty does not mean we are to be brutal or needlessly cruel. It means we are to live and speak the truth filled with mercy and love, not concealing or covering up actions and intents.

Be honest with God. Honesty brings us first of all to the plain truth that we all have sinned: "For all have sinned; all fall short of God's glorious standard" (Rom. 3:23). Honesty begins with admitting that I am a sinner in need of redemption and grace. But the beauty of being "honest with God" is that it leads to repentance; and repentance leads to forgiveness; and forgiveness leads to renewed trust and love.

Be honest with myself. What at first seems too painful and difficult is really a gift and the basis for all other relationships in life, particularly marriage. Being honest means I must quit pretending I've got it all together, quit pretending I'm perfect. When I start by being honest with myself, God can meet my deepest needs. Honesty can be scary because it's like getting close to a canyon's edge, and we avoid it at all costs. What we must be assured of is that being honest with God is a safe place. We can "take the leap," knowing He is

there. And if I truly know that God is meeting my needs, that takes the pressure off my marriage. I am not so desperate to be loved, to be accepted by my spouse. I can love more freely, with no strings or hidden agendas.

Be honest with my spouse. It is in the transparency of honesty that the integrity of a marriage is built and strengthened. We can play games with words and learn to hide behind them, argue with them, strengthen our position with them, even tell lies with them. But truthfulness comes when we are honest and open with each other.

Nothing reveals us as marriage does. Within the context of a committed marriage, we have the opportunity to be truly known. Outside of a marriage, we can keep up a good appearance, but within marriage, our souls are laid bare—we are exposed for who we are. Integrity and truthfulness within marriage are like having a solid foundation under a house. Lies and deceit within a marriage are like having termites infesting your house—it's bound to eventually crumble. Dishonesty destroys trust, and if ever trust is needed within a relationship, it's within marriage.

Honesty can either promote or destroy intimacy. Our spouse doesn't need to hear every thought and urge we've ever had. We must discern what is profitable to speak and what is not. Truth is a delicate power, and it's often difficult to understand how to wield it. We

Honesty

can carelessly slash with the truth and in the process wound our loved one. Effective truth is like a surgeon's tool; one must know how to use it. Wisdom must prevail. Truth told with love and kindness gains a hearing.

Honesty builds trust, anust promotes intimacy. Jamie and Mike had a problem communicating. She tended to keep her feelings bottled up and would simmer inside with resentment over the way Mike spoke to her at times. She told us, "Last week he did it again. He made a remark that really hurt my feelings. But instead of what I usually did—keep my feelings of anger and rejection inside—I calmly told him the truth." Mike was surprised and appreciated Jamie's honesty, and instead of driving them apart, it actually drew them together.

In certain areas it's best to be completely honest. In financial matters, tell each other the truth right from the beginning. Be honest about time—exactly where you're going, why you're going, who you're going with. Be honest about keeping your promises. A marriage built on anything less than the truth is built on a shaky foundation.

Lord, I pray that first of all I will be honest with You. Forgive and cleanse me, Lord, of all unrighteous thoughts and deeds. I confess my utter dependence on You. I pray that I will learn from Your Word how to build my marriage with honesty and integrity. May I be a person of my word, and may I learn what it means to speak the truth—covered with love—to my spouse. Amen.

REFLECTION

"Truthfulness means that, when you talk, you make a most careful bridge of your words. This requires two cares, really: care for the topic, to get it right; and care for your spouse, that she or he hears it right."

Walter Wangerin, *As for Me and My House*

"Far too many Christians do not deal honestly with their lives. Clichés about the power of the Word are repeated with smug piety among people who see little evidence of its life-changing impact. . . . It is much easier to tell a depressed friend to spend more time in prayer than to grapple with his life. The pathway to change is more often discussed and debated than displayed. Three things keep me from cynically giving up on the hope of finding life-changing reality in Christ: Scripture, the Holy Spirit, and a few people."

Larry Crabb, *Inside Out*

LET'S TALK ABOUT IT

1 How honest are you with your spouse? In what areas do you need to be more honest?

2 Is it possible to damage your relationship with the truth? How can withholding truth damage your marriage?

YOUR NOTES/REFLECTIONS/PRAYERS/GOALS

_____

_____

_____

_____

_____

_____

_____

_____

_____

_____

_____

_____

Honesty

TENDERNESS

34

Be kind to one another, tenderhearted, forgiving one another,

just as God in Christ forgave you.

Ephesians 4:32, NKJV

PRAYER

Lord, I do want to be tender to my spouse. But so often I find myself thinking about my own needs, my own hurts. Teach me tenderness and kindness. As I study Your character and nature in Your Word, I can see Your compassion and tenderness to others. Help me to mirror Your character in my relationship to my spouse. May I be slow to get angry and quick to forgive. In Jesus' name, amen.

"Your own soul is nourished when you are kind, but you destroy yourself when you are cruel" (Prov. 11:17).

INSIGHT

Bill and I were discussing marriage with our friends Steve and Cindy. We were talking about the needs all of us have in marriage, and I remarked that I believed women needed tenderness and kindness. Steve, a type-A high-achiever, interjected, "We men need tenderness, too. I don't think women know how much we really do need it." Somehow that surprised me and shook my stereotype a little. But the more I think about it, the more I believe Steve is right, and Bill agrees with him. We all need tenderness.

The theologian Martin Buber wrote a classic book about how people perceive one another. In *I and Thou,* he describes how some people see others as objects--*I* and *It,* rather than *I* and *Thou*—*thou* meaning a significant being created by God. When we view others God has placed in our lives with love and see them with His eyes, we will see them tenderly, with compassion. This is part of Jesus' greatest teaching—to love one another as He loves us.

How simple, how profound. And yet how extremely hard it can be at times to treat one another with tenderness. Why is that so, knowing it's one of the most important callings of our lives? Because we are human. We grow tired, impatient. Sometimes we don't

feel well. We may have problems from our past, and we have our own set of needs.

When our busy lives require much of us, we often need our spouses to help make our lives work. Financial commitments, household chores, children, ministry, and social involvements fill our calendars. We can begin to regard one another as commodities— objects—rather than a precious, God-created soul with whom we share the journey of life.

Tenderness and kindness are wonderful qualities. They really define love. Yes, there are some days it's easier to be impatient with our spouse than to be tender. Not long ago, I was in a minor car accident. I was upset that I had another ding in my car and that we would have to spend quite a bit of money to repair it. But Bill's response meant more to me than I can say. He said tenderly, "I'm sorry about the accident and the car. But I'm glad I still have you."

When I think of tenderness, I think of expressions. I think of eye contact, how we look at one another. I think of words, how we say them. I think of grace, how we respond to each other. We have frequent opportunities to be angry. But we must use anger wisely, knowing that rage can blow up

Tenderness

the bridges that connect us. We must be gentle with each other and honor each other with the gift of tenderness. It is a gift that means much. It is easy in marriage to forget to be tender. We can get in a hurry with each other, and tenderness gets lost.

In one of his letters, the apostle Paul challenges us to the kind of behavior that will knit spouses together: "Therefore, as the elect of God, holy and beloved, put on tender mercies, kindness, humility, meekness, longsuffering; bearing with one another, and forgiving one another, if anyone has a complaint against another; even as Christ forgave you, so you also must do. But above all these things put on love, which is the bond of perfection. And let the peace of God rule in your hearts, to which also you were called in one body; and be thankful" (Col. 3:12-15, NKJV).

Lord, thank You for Your example of tenderness and kindness. You saw people—really saw them—and loved them. May we display that quality to one another in our marriage. May our words be tempered with grace, our expressions with love, and our behavior with tenderness. Amen.

REFLECTION

"Sweet thoughts, kind whispers, a listening ear, and a helping hand—these are the things that speak your beloved's language. No special setting can take the place of word and deed given from the heart. Life is short and we have never too much time for gladdening the hearts of those who travel the way with us. Oh, be swift to love! Make haste to be kind."

Henri F. Amiel, quoted in *Quiet Moments for Couples*

"Compassion is the sometimes fatal capacity for feeling what it is like to live inside somebody else's skin. It is the knowledge that there can never really be any peace and joy for me until there is peace and joy finally for you too."

Frederick Buechner, *Wishful Thinking*

1 Discuss ways that each of you can show more tenderness toward the other.

2 Make a conscious effort to speak and look with tenderness to your spouse at least once a day, and take note of the effect.

YOUR NOTES/REFLECTIONS/PRAYERS/GOALS

_____

_____

_____

_____

_____

_____

_____

_____

_____

_____

_____

_____

_____

Tenderness

LOYALTY

35

A friend is always loyal.

Proverbs 17:17

PRAYER

Lord, there are many opportunities in our culture to be unfaithful, to be pulled away from each other. Thank You for reminding us that fidelity is important to You. Keep us faithful to one another. Keep us devoted to one another. May our marriage be filled with a strong loyalty that will protect our marriage bond. Amen.

SCRIPTURE

"Loyalty makes a person attractive" (Prov. 19:22).

Loyalty within a marriage is the glue, the bond that holds us together. It is an essential attitude, and there are several ways to recognize it.

Loyalty means being true, forsaking all other lovers. It reminds me of the card I gave Bill for Valentine's Day. On the outside was a picture of the earth, with this statement below: "There are almost 6 billion people on the planet." And inside the card, it expressed what I feel: "And you're my favorite one." When I married Bill, he became "my favorite one," my only one. When I married him, I forsook the pursuit and romantic attention of all others, even in thought.

Don had an attractive, capable secretary who meant a lot to him. She occupied the office space right outside his door. Over time, Don's wife, Susan, grew uneasy about his relationship with his secretary. Susan was not normally the jealous type, but when she confessed her insecurities to Don, he moved his secretary's desk to another area to affirm his loyalty to Susan.

Loyalty means making one another a priority. Loyalty truly is an attitude, a stubborn resolve to make my relationship with my spouse a top priority, right up there after loving God. It's important to give one another our best, not leftover dregs. In years past, I have had to repent of my overcrowded schedule. Being loyal to my spouse means not becoming

overcommitted to things that take us away from each other. It means caring about the things my loved one cares about.

Loyalty means defending one another, believing we are a team. We have watched the teamwork in the marriage of our friends Bob and Caro. They are both gifted and strong people. He is a physician with a busy practice, and she has been a teacher and is active in the community. Even though their giftedness is in different areas, they work to defend and assist each other in their various schedules and responsibilities. Loyalty means being on the same team, going the same direction, supporting each other.

Loyalty means being there for each other through all seasons and conditions. Our friends Paul and Leta have had many good years of pastoring and of raising their children. Now that these responsibilities are done and life should be easier, they are dealing with Paul's multiple sclerosis. It is hard for both of them, in separate ways. Leta is fiercely loyal, despite the changes in Paul's physical abilities, and it is an inspiration to be with them and observe their undying love and loyalty toward one another.

Other friends, Joan and Bob, have a different situation. Bob has to do a lot of travel for his work, but Joan is terrified of flying. She has tried many times and miserably failed. Out of loyalty to Joan, Bob tries to schedule as many driving trips as he can so she can go with him. Out of loyalty to Bob, Joan is doing some personal therapy to try to get over this fear so she can be able to fly with him. Loyalty often involves sacrifice.

Loyalty does not betray confidence or trust. To be loyal to my loved one means to use discretion about what I say about my spouse to even my siblings, parents, and best friends. There are certain matters that are private—sacred—between a husband and a wife. If I am careless about these matters in talking about them to others, it destroys an important level of trust in our marriage.

I maintain loyalty to Bill by the way I talk about him to our children, to my friends. Loyalty also means not making each other the brunt of jokes when with other couples. The story may be funny to everyone else, but more often than not, it smacks of betrayal to

the spouse who is the object of everyone's laughter. When we tell about some blunder, flaw, or mistake our spouse made, even when done in humor, we may be committing a form of betrayal that feels disloyal to our spouse.

Is it possible to be too loyal? To be foolish in defending our spouse? Only if he or she asks you to violate your convictions, commit a sin, or do something wrong. You can say no in those circumstances and still be loyal. The apostle Paul tells us that true love "is not rude" and "always protects."

Lord, we praise You for Your faithfulness, Your loyalty to us. Teach us this important concept so that we may love one another with a deep, lasting, and faithful love. May we be sensitive to any intrusions that would come between us and separate our love. Amen.

REFLECTION

"In marriages, faithfulness is a symbol of commitment. It is a statement that our heart belongs to our spouse. This loyalty takes precedence over all other allegiances—parents, relatives, coworkers, and friends of each gender. Faithfulness insists that we allow no one to compete with this special place of affection."

Steve Stephens, *Experience the Best*

"Love is expressed unequivocally in . . . the availability offered. The assurance that each will be there for the other when needed, when expected, when desired is the confidence of being loved."

David Augsburger, *Sustaining Love*

1. Define for each other what loyalty means in the context of your relationship. Do you feel "first" with your spouse?

2. Discuss practical ways you can improve your loyalty toward one another in setting priorities, defending one another, and supporting each other.

YOUR NOTES/REFLECTIONS/PRAYERS/GOALS

_____

_____

_____

_____

_____

_____

_____

_____

_____

_____

_____

_____

_____

_____

_____

Loyalty

TRUST

36

Trust in the Lord with all your heart; do not depend on your own understanding.

Seek his will in all you do, and he will direct your paths.

Proverbs 3:5-6

PRAYER

Lord, what an important quality is trust in a relationship! We have so much to learn about this. Father, in our humanity and our failings, we often do not give one another good reasons to trust. But You, Lord, are worthy of trust, and as we trust You—throwing the whole weight of our lives upon You—we pray that we will learn what it means to build this quality into our relationship so that it will be an integral part of our lives together. Amen.

SCRIPTURE

"Bear one another's burdens, and so fulfill the law of Christ" (Gal. 6:2, NKJV).

Bill and I had much to learn about trust when we first married, although we didn't immediately recognize it. I had never successfully managed a checking account before I married, and I proceeded to overdraw our account many times. Bill, true to his sense of humor, often would embarrass me in front of friends by disclosing some personal facts between us. It got a laugh, but I was hurt. As we grew to be able to talk to one another about these matters, we began to work through them. We realized that trust is like building a cornerstone in our relationship. It was a process. Bill was slow to trust me again with the checkbook after a few disasters. I was reluctant to trust him with some feelings after he had publicly teased me about something I had considered private.

So we would regroup and confront one another. We tried to listen. We asked for forgiveness. Then we would start the dance again. Extending ourselves again. Trusting again. Trying the ice again. Would it hold? Was it more solid this time?

Trust doesn't happen easily, overnight. We find in our marriage that the process of trust must be constantly reevaluated, protected, and redefined. We have grown to trust each other because our love has been tried. In his book *Love Life for Every Married Couple,* Ed Wheat wrote, "Intimacy can grow only in a place of safety. When husband and wife are afraid of hurt, rebuff, criticism, and misunderstanding,

they will find it difficult to touch and share freely. So if you want real intimacy in your marriage, you will have to establish trust in your relationship."

Trust is built on caring and consideration. Trust is built through days, weeks, and years of learning about the other, of choosing to believe the best. Trust means providing support for one another in reaching for goals, offering understanding in hard times, simply being a sounding board. To trust means to have confidence in the integrity, ability, and character of a person.

Trust is earned. Trust is one of the most empowering qualities in a good marriage. Someone once said, "Love is a given, but trust and respect are earned." I think there is truth to this. Most of us go into marriage trusting our spouse. But trust can be eroded when we are deceitful and manipulative.

Trust is being vulnerable. We are hesitant to be vulnerable with someone we cannot trust. When I tell my husband I trust him, I am saying that I have confidence in his truthfulness, his fidelity, his keeping my confidences, and his love for me. Trust is a two-way street, and good marriages have reciprocal trust.

Trust must be protected. When a wife tells me in marriage counseling that she can no longer trust her husband because of betrayal, I find this the most difficult thing to overcome in the relationship. Often trust never returns. When trust is destroyed, the relationship is usually destroyed with it.

But outright betrayal is not the only way in which trust can be eroded. Trust weakens when one spouse attacks the other's decisions. Trust is undermined when one spouse fights over trivial things like who's right about which is the shortest route to a friend's house. If you find that trust about serious issues has been broken in your marriage, seek professional Christian counseling. Do everything you can to protect and nurture trust.

Trust is forged over time. It always takes longer to build trust than to destroy it. A trust that has taken years to forge can be threatened by one hour's irresponsible behavior. Take seriously the need to build trust with your spouse. Trust creates an atmosphere of safety, a feeling that I can be myself with my spouse, that it's all right to be vulnerable with him or her.

Trust is risky. It involves unconditional love, which of course is what Jesus did for us on the cross. He simply stretched out His arms and said, "I love you." We can do the same for one another.

Lord, we want to learn what it means to trust You more. We want to throw the full weight of ourselves—our plans, our marriage, and all that we have and are—on You. And then may we learn more of this fragile but essential quality of trust with each other. Teach us to earn trust. Teach us to treasure it, to protect it. And teach us to give it, knowing we can always trust You. Amen.

REFLECTION

"Trust is awakened in us. Trust is not taught, it is caught. We come into being and grow only within affirming, trusting relationships. We cannot know ourselves apart from another's belief in us now and in what we can become. What's more, it is only upon another's affirmation of our worth that we acquire a capacity to affirm others. This give-and-take begins in childhood and continues for a lifetime."

Ira J. Tannger, *Trust*

"The point of marriage is not to create a quick commonality by tearing down all boundaries; on the contrary, a good marriage is one in which each partner appoints the other to be the guardian of his solitude, and thus they show each other the greatest possible trust."

Robert Hass and Stephen Miller, *Into the Garden*

LET'S TALK ABOUT IT

1 Ask each other, "Are we having difficulty trusting each other? In what area? Why?"

2 Tell each other, "I want to trust you more in this area, but I need your help. Will you listen to how I feel?"

YOUR NOTES/REFLECTIONS/PRAYERS/GOALS

_____

_____

_____

_____

_____

_____

_____

_____

_____

_____

_____

_____

_____

_____

Trust

PRAYING FOR THE PRESENCE OF GOD IN OUR HOME ATMOSPHERE

Optimism

Children's Lives

Hospitality

Celebrations

Harmony

Good Humor

PART 7

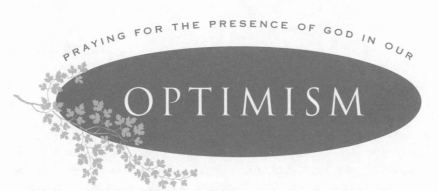

OPTIMISM

37

Whatever things are true, whatever things are noble, whatever things are just, whatever things are pure, whatever things are lovely, whatever things are of good report, if there is any virtue and if there is anything praiseworthy— meditate on these things.

Philippians 4:8, NKJV

PRAYER

Lord, it is often the smallest thing that seems to reduce us to two arguing children who want their own way. Help us to discipline ourselves to look for the good, to look for the positive. Forgive us for being negative. Thank You for reminding us that in an atmosphere of praise, people thrive. Amen.

"The Lord is my light and my salvation—so why should I be afraid? . . . I am confident that I will see the Lord's goodness while I am here in the land of the living" (Ps. 27:1, 13).

Everyone needs hope, and I (Bill) really needed it the other day. I walked into the house, discouraged over a canceled parenting seminar I was supposed to lead. A several-thousand-member church had anticipated the attendance of a large group of young parents, and I was looking forward to it. They had printed eight hundred tickets and told me to ship enough books for a minimum of five hundred people. Two days before the event, the embarrassed pastor called and told me that due to conflicts, only thirty people had signed up. We agreed to cancel the seminar, even though I had ordered and sent thousands of dollars' worth of books to sell at the book table, books that were nonreturnable to my publisher. The pastor was shipping them back to me. No honorarium, no seminar fee, only a very large invoice for books.

I sank down on the sofa and with a big sigh told Nancie, "That's it. I think I'm going to quit trying to do these seminars." Nancie gave me an understanding hug and then reminded me of my last seminar and how successful it had been. Her optimism helped me overcome my disappointment and personal "pity party."

It is so true that within marriage we need to focus on the positive rather than the negative. In fact, it is crucial to a healthy marriage. When we first marry, most of us have a strong sense of optimism about the future. It doesn't take long to discover that we've married an imperfect human being, with his or her own set of flaws. Our expectations can be dashed if each partner begins to focus on the negative aspects of the other. It can be tempting to major on the negative, and, like chickens in a pen, to pick on the weak chicken.

In his letter to the Corinthian church, the apostle Paul inspires us to optimism. He reminds us that "Love never gives up, never loses faith, is always hopeful, and endures through every circumstance" (1 Cor. 13:7). That's what Nancie's optimism did for me.

Loving optimism can also help us endure difficult circumstances. Our dear editor, Lynn Vanderzalm, suffers from chronic fatigue syndrome, an immune-system disorder that leaves her fatigued and debilitated. When she and her daughter first became ill ten years ago, they were nearly bedridden for several years. Because medical science is still mysti-

Optimism

fied about what causes the illness and how it can be effectively treated, it is easy to become discouraged about the future. The chronic illness of a spouse could cause a lot of erosion in a marriage. But Lynn and her husband, Bas, are not letting Lynn's illness cause them to become negative. When Nancie and I have been with them, we have sensed their hope, joy, and a belief that life is essentially good, in spite of the stresses and limitations this illness has placed on them.

Optimistic love can carry us a long way through the circumstances of life. Jesus, sensing his disciples' discouragement before He left them, reminds them, "Let not your heart be troubled. You are trusting God, now trust in me. There are many homes up there where my Father lives, and I am going to prepare them for your coming. When everything is ready, then I will come and get you, so that you can always be with me where I am" (John 14:1-3, TLB).

When your spouse suffers a setback, you can help by focusing on the bright side. Or you can further entrench your spouse's depression or fear by being negative. Words are powerful. I am not suggesting that you completely ignore the problem or deny that it exists. This can be equally damaging because ignoring the problem tends to take us away from reality or invalidate real feelings. It can also evade dealing with the problem.

But remind each other that there is always hope! When we focus on hope rather than despair, we are living with holy optimism. Think about it: faith takes optimism; hope takes optimism; even love takes a good dose of optimism. Knowing that God is always there, never leaving or forsaking us, that He loves us no matter what, is the most optimistic truth in all the universe.

Lord Jesus, You and Your Father are the essence of hope. We ask that You give us this sense of Your hope. Help us to see that optimism is a big part of hope and that hope is the key to joy and peace. Help us to focus our eyes on hope rather than despair, on good rather than evil, on opportunities rather than obstacles. In Your holy name, amen.

Optimism

REFLECTION

"Lord, make me an instrument of Your peace. Where there is hatred, let me sow love; where there is injury, pardon; where there is doubt, faith; where there is despair, hope; where there is darkness, light; and where there is sadness, joy."

St. Francis of Assisi

"The optimist proclaims that we live in the best of all possible worlds;
and the pessimist fears this is true."

James Branch Cabell, "The Silver Stallion"

LET'S TALK ABOUT IT

1 How can you use optimism to love and serve your spouse?

2 Make a list of the positive things, the possibilities in your life right now. Also write down your hopes and dreams. Share these with your spouse.

YOUR NOTES/REFLECTIONS/PRAYERS/GOALS

_____

_____

_____

_____

_____

_____

_____

_____

_____

_____

_____

Optimism

CHILDREN'S LIVES

38

· · · · · · · · · · · · · · · · ·

I prayed for this child, and the Lord has granted me what I asked of him. So now I give him to the Lord. For his whole life he will be given over to the Lord.

1 Samuel 1:27-28, NIV

PRAYER

Lord, we want our children to know You. We give our children back to You just as Samuel's mother did. We ask You to give us wisdom in raising our children. Thank You for entrusting us with these precious lives. They will be in our care for a few years, but in Your care forever, and we acknowledge your Lordship in their lives. Amen.

SCRIPTURE

"Behold, children are a legacy from the Lord; the fruit of the womb is His reward. As arrows in the hand of a mighty man, so are the children of one's youth" (Ps. 127:3-4, MLB).

Parenting has an enormous effect on marriage. Until a couple brings a child into their family, they have no idea how much children change the dynamics of a marriage. When children join the family, the time and affection spouses normally gave to each other must be shared with little people who can be demanding. There is an amazing amount of work involved with children, and yet parenting is a joy that most of us would do again if life repeated itself.

The book you are reading is a sequel to our book *Lord, Bless My Child: A Keepsake Prayer Journal to Pray for the Character of God in My Child.* That book is dedicated to the concept of praying for our children's lives. Nancie and I discovered one day that our prayers for our children were repetitious. We often prayed for their physical safety, for little sniffles, and for other childhood problems they faced. But we realized that God had a much bigger agenda for our children than just keeping them safe and well. God wanted to develop His character in the lives of our children. So we began to pray bigger prayers, prayers of faith and vision and power.

I believe that every parent and every grandparent is called to stand in the gap for their children and grandchildren. There is no middle ground here. A New Testament story tells of a father who had a son possessed by demons. The disciples tried to pray for this boy, but they saw no results. The father had

every right to give up at that moment, but he was persistent. Later, as he saw Jesus approaching, surrounded by a great crowd of people, he cried out to Jesus and asked him to heal his son (see Luke 9:37-43). What strikes me is that no one else in this crowd would have approached Jesus on behalf of this tormented boy. No one! If this father had not been persistent, this boy would never have been delivered. But because of the father's persistence, his son was completely healed.

It is important for us to pray for our children (and grandchildren) because we are the only ones who are really called to do so. There are no professional child prayer warriors we can hire to do the praying for us. No other human being cares about our kids' lives as much as we do. Why do we pray?

We pray because we love our children. Bathing our children in intercessory prayer is a powerful way to express our love for them. They will not necessarily thank us for this. They may not even recognize prayer's power at the time. But someday we will be able to look back and see the hand of God moving because of our prayers.

We pray in obedience to God's Word. You and I are called to pray. Some people quit when they do not see the desired results. But if we are truly obedient to God, we will continue to "pray without ceasing."

We pray because we live in difficult times. Our children face the negative influences of friends, school, the media, and a thousand other places. An unseen spiritual battle is waging, and the minds of our children are at stake. When you pray for your children, you are building a spiritual hedge around their lives.

We pray because prayer does make a difference. The Bible teaches us that "the earnest prayer of a righteous person has great power and wonderful results" (James 5:16). When you pray, you are using a powerful tool to enact the powers of heaven to work on your behalf. Prayer works.

Pray *for* your children, and pray *with* them. Pray for them in the morning; pray with them at night. Pray at the dinner table; pray at their bedside. Pray long intercessory prayers; pray short quickies.

Pray for their friends, teachers, associates, dating partners, and the unknown person they will someday marry. Pray for their physical, mental, spiritual, and emotional needs. Pray for attitudes, habits, thought life, and con-

duct. Pray for their heroes, music, mentors, and their idols. Pray for protection from drugs, pornography, ungodly philosophy, evil music, lust, fornication, vanity, and pride. Pray about what they see, hear, and touch. Pray for them before a test, before a game. Breathe a prayer for them every time they walk out the door. Pray for their choices, character, appetites, and dreams. Pray for their giftedness and their weaknesses. Pray for their salvation and for a divine calling for their lives. Pray that they will become kingdom builders, mighty men and women of God, men and women of compassion and wisdom, filled with God's power and Holy Spirit. And when you have prayed for all of that, do it again. Never stop praying for your kids.

Lord, we know what we parents need to do. Give us the will, the courage, the determination, the discipline, and the wisdom to pray. We ask You to invade our lives and our children's lives with Your presence. Help us to be faithful in this vital ministry. In Jesus' name, amen.

REFLECTION

"So, awed by the beauty and goodness of our children, dumbfounded by our failure to be the parents we hoped to be, worshiping, giving horsey rides, and picking up peas, we are brought to our knees. It is a good idea to learn to pray. As the atom is smashed to release tremendous physical energy, so through prayer we smash the limits of personal power for good and ill."

Polly Berrien Berends, *Gently Lead*

"I believe I need to pray for my children: for their salvation, for their protection, for the development of their characters. But I also need to pray for the people who influence them daily: their teachers, their peers, their closest friends, and me."

Karen Scalf Linamen, *The Parent Warrior*

LET'S TALK ABOUT IT

1. If you have children (and grandchildren), make a list of the things you need to pray about on their behalf. Now begin to pray that list daily.

2. Praying for children is one area of prayer most married couples can agree on. It is a good place to begin praying out loud with each other as a couple because the focus is on your children rather than on each other.

YOUR NOTES/REFLECTIONS/PRAYERS/GOALS

_____

_____

_____

_____

_____

_____

_____

_____

_____

_____

_____

Children's Lives

HOSPITALITY

39

In the house of the righteous there is much treasure.

Proverbs 15:6, NKJV

PRAYER

Lord, we want our home to be a safe place—a place of peace, a place where others can come to relax and be renewed. Help us to consciously foster an atmosphere that is like a sanctuary to us, to our children, and to others who need hope and healing. Forgive us for false expectations of what a home should be, and help us to remember the qualities that You—our eternal home—give us. Amen.

SCRIPTURE

"Be glad for all God is planning for you. . . . When God's children are in need, be the one to help them out. And get into the habit of inviting guests home for dinner or, if they need lodging, for the night"
(Rom. 12:12-13).

Bill and I want to offer hospitality to people, but sometimes I have been intimidated to have people to our house because I worry about things being "good" enough. Our home is not something out of a decorator magazine, and while I love Martha Stewart, she would never do a feature from my kitchen.

But in Bill's and my varied lifestyle of pastoring and then publishing and being surrounded by family and friends, we've come to realize that everyone needs hospitality. Everyone likes to feel wanted, welcomed. We want our children, family, and friends to feel comfortable when they walk in the door. Hospitality means giving; it means extending ourselves. And yet the benefits are worth it. Through hospitality we strengthen relationships and build friendships. And we are better people for learning how to give from our home. My mother-in-law declares her house is always "happy" after company leaves. She says it's smiling with a certain warmth or glow. Maybe what we feel is really our own joy from giving and sharing.

The other day I came home from an overnight trip and tried to look with new eyes at our house, as a visitor would see it. Our house is comfortable and casual; it's unmistakably a family house, the kind of place where you don't think twice about putting your feet up on the ottoman. *Functional* is definitely a key word. Most of the furnishings in our house are common, ordinary couches,

end tables, and lamps. They are practical and well used.

As you think about offering hospitality from your home, remember that hospitality is more an atmosphere than an appearance. It doesn't depend on what we *have* as much as who we *are*. When we give hospitality to others, we give love and warmth and welcome, not just rooms and food.

As you evaluate your hospitality, think about these questions:

Is your home a place to relax? Are you and your family relaxed in your home, or are you fussy and fidgety? Do others feel at ease in your house? When you are relaxed, others around you will feel free to relax too. Is your home clean enough to be healthy yet messy enough to be happy? Can people relax emotionally in your home? Have you learned what it means to keep confidence and allow others to be vulnerable?

Is your home a place of nourishment? The kitchen is the heart of the home, the place where we offer nourishing food and drink, restoring energy we've expended. There is something very heartwarming about walking into a home and smelling the fragrance of a simmering stew or seeing a table set with lit candles. The scene says, "This is for you because I care about your needs. I have been planning for you to come because you are loved and wanted here." These simple acts of attending to basic needs can be profound statements of love and acceptance.

Is your home a place of peace? Peace means there is order and harmony that arises from an underlying sense of discipline in the function and design of your home. But peace is much more than design, color, or furniture; real peace comes from the people who live there. Life is full of cares, and it's easy to lose peace. What makes a home a shelter rather than a prison? It is an atmosphere of safety, peace, and love.

Is your home a place that allows interruptions? I've learned that often the most important things in our lives are not on the calendar. Instead, they often come on ordinary days. It may be an interruption, an unexpected visitor, an inconvenience, a surprise. In spite of our elaborate plans and schemes, real life happens. This is when you can use your creativity to make your home truly hospitable.

Is your home a place where your guests will see God's presence? As God becomes more and more at home in our lives, others who come into our homes will sense His presence. We can make a conscious effort to celebrate Him by the music we play, the type of entertainment we watch, and the reading material that is available. Even through the tone of our conversations, we can honor His unseen presence, helping to set an atmosphere where His presence is evident to all who come into our homes.

Hospitality means opening our hearts and homes to others, sharing with them what we have. Often we confuse *entertaining* with *hospitality*. Entertainment is more of a production designed to impress. Hospitality is a gift we give to others. It is relaxed, real, and spontaneous. Practice this kind of hospitality with your family, friends, and other guests.

Help us remember, Lord, that even a cup of water in Your name is an act of love and hospitality to those in need. Help us to be the kind of couple that others want to be with because we have learned how to pour love, acceptance, joy, and blessing into their lives. Let our home be a citadel of Your grace, and crown it with Your joyful, loving presence. In Jesus' name, amen.

REFLECTION

"The place where you live is the place where you will have the most opportunities to serve the Lord by serving others."

Mother Teresa, quoted in *The Best Things Ever Said about Parenting*

"In the end, memories have much more power than decor."

Baroness Raffaello de Banfield, quoted in *Architectural Digest*

1. As a couple, how do you show hospitality to others? In what ways can you grow in offering hospitality?

2. Think of the people and homes that have offered you the warmest hospitality. What made the experience good for you? How can you emulate that quality?

YOUR NOTES/REFLECTIONS/PRAYERS/GOALS

_____

_____

_____

_____

_____

_____

_____

_____

_____

_____

_____

_____

_____

_____

Hospitality

CELEBRATIONS

40

The joy of the Lord is your strength!

Nehemiah 8:10

PRAYER

You are a joyful God, and we want to be joyful people. Help us to be people of celebration and laughter. Lord, may we celebrate our very life together, not just on anniversaries, but daily . . . our marriage, our children, and Your goodness. Remind us, Lord, to create surprises and celebratory moments with our spouse. Help us to be positive and uplifting in a way that encourages and enriches our spouse. May we be beacons of hope, light, and joy to those around us. Amen.

SCRIPTURE

"Then I heard again what sounded like the shouting of a huge crowd. . . . 'Praise the Lord. For the Lord our God, the Almighty, reigns. Let us be glad and rejoice and honor him; for the time has come for the wedding banquet of the Lamb, and his bride has prepared herself'" (Rev. 19:6-7, TLB).

Celebrations

Celebration in marriage is like having frequent new beginnings. It provides an atmosphere where love and forgiveness can take place. Celebration makes life fun. Billy Graham once said, "I want to be remembered as a person who was fun to live with." Life without celebration is like a dry well—promising something it cannot deliver.

Every marriage needs a sense of joy and happiness to survive the storms of life. If your marriage consists only of the mundane—bills, kids, garbage, chores, arguments, and watching TV—then you are missing out. You have lost your spark. Forging a strong marriage is not easy. It can be hard work. But if you're building a truly great project, you press on with the dream of what can be. And once the project is completed, you think, *What if I'd quit back there when it was so rough? I would have missed this!* Celebrations, large and small, help us complete the project of building a strong marriage.

Nancie and I love taking minivacations to the coast or some other place where we can just be alone and shower affection on each other. Every once in a while, just as you celebrate the Fourth of July, you need to have fireworks go off in your marriage. You need to plan another special memory between the two of you to keep the spark alive in your relationship.

It's possible to miss real life while slogging through the one you have. Too often we put off celebration so we can do the routine things we think will bring us contentment and happiness. We plod through, thinking someday we will feel better, laugh more, enjoy each other. It's important to celebrate now. After Nancie's father died, her mother told us, "Celebrate along the way. We were always going to take a little trip, to do things we somehow had never done because we thought we would have time later. Do them now."

God was into celebration. The book of Revelation tells us that the end of this age and the crowning event of the beginning of eternity will be punctuated with a celebration of the marriage supper of the Lamb. We cannot be the people God intends us to be without a sense of celebration. And He celebrates with us daily through magnificent sunrises and sunsets, through the explosive colors of flowers, through the choruses of birds.

When thinking of celebration, we often think about an organized event such as a birthday, an anniversary, a job promotion—and these are all important. But there is a much deeper meaning to celebration. We need to celebrate people. When you celebrate another person, you are saying to that person, "You are very, very special." This is especially true with our spouse. When you celebrate your spouse, you are giving him or her the special attention that only you can give. It is expressed in laughing together, going out to dinner, having secret names for each other, seeing the twinkle in each other's eyes, giving each other frequent surprises, sending cards or flowers, and making midday intimate phone calls. But the essence of celebrating your spouse says that he or she is of the utmost importance and significance to you, and to God.

When I celebrate Nancie as a person, it means I cherish her. I adore her. It means I light up when I see her walk into a room. It means I delight in watching her interact with other people or complete a project or care for one of our children. Sometimes I need to simply come home from work, look into her eyes, and ask her how she is doing. My eyes tell her I care. My expression tells her that I adore her. My attention tells her that I love her.

We practice this kind of celebration in a conscious way. We can all find it easy to slip into the routine of jobs, meals, bills, housework, and commute time and forget to add the spice of joy and surprise to our relationship. Celebration becomes a habit only after we consciously practice it frequently.

Hey! Why not kidnap your spouse, go rent a red convertible, put the top down, and go somewhere, anywhere? Go park somewhere. Do something crazy. Do something unforgettable to celebrate one another.

Lord, help us to be people who know how to celebrate life, Your grace, and each other. Put our work and mission in perspective. Help us to make joy and laugher a priority. In Jesus' name, amen.

REFLECTION

"It is important in our lives and work that we celebrate our little victories as they come. If we wait for something major to celebrate, we will miss much of the potential joy in our lives. I believe it is the overworked, under-rewarded men and women who reach midlife and look up one day to ask, 'Is that all there is?'"

Claire Cloninger, *When God Shines Through*

"Work is fine, but when it's mixed with fun, it's a lot better. Don't be a fun pauper. Get into the delights a good God has put into the world."

Norman Vincent Peale, quoted in *The Best Things Ever Said about Parenting*

1 Everyone struggles with limited time and resources in life and marriage, but think back to times when you feel you celebrated your marriage. What did you do that made it special?

2 List two goals that you have for learning to celebrate your marriage. What steps can you take to reach these goals?

YOUR NOTES/REFLECTIONS/PRAYERS/GOALS

Celebrations

PRAYING FOR THE PRESENCE OF GOD IN OUR

HARMONY

41

Better to live on a corner of the roof than share a house with a quarrelsome [spouse].

Proverbs 21:9, NIV

PRAYER

Lord, I so want our home to be a place of joy, with an atmosphere of peace. Remind me to sing, Father. Help me, Lord, to be quick to see the lovely, to affirm the positive, to compliment often. May each of us do all we can in our own attitudes to make our home a shelter of Your grace. Amen.

SCRIPTURE

"How wonderful it is, how pleasant, when [we] live in harmony! For harmony is as precious as the fragrant anointing oil that was poured over Aaron's head and ran down onto his beard and onto the border of his robe. Harmony is as refreshing as the dew on Mount Hermon, on the mountains of Israel. . . . even life forevermore" (Ps. 133:1-3, TLB).

Harmony

As I (Bill) was writing this chapter, my telephone rang. I picked it up, and a deep voice on the other end said, "Is this Bill Carmichael, class of '64?" I knew it must be one of my long-lost classmates, but I had no clue as to who. Within minutes he was at my office, and we were catching up on the thirty-plus years that had passed between us without contact.

I remembered him as a student body leader with a strong call of God on his life. He and his wife were the kind of rock-solid people you knew would be successful at steadily building the kingdom of God. But I was surprised when he told me he and his wife had, at one point in their ministry, split up. "For two years I pastored alone. My wife couldn't take it anymore and left." *You two? Mr. and Mrs. Steady-as-a-Rock?* I thought to myself. He did not elaborate much on what it was she "couldn't take," but I suspect it was the same things that many of us get weary about in our marriages. He said they were both stubborn, wanting their own way, and endured years of the same old arguments.

But his face lit up as he went on to tell me that they had gotten back together and were now happier than ever. "What caused you to finally get back together?" I asked.

Without hesitation he said, "Both of us became willing to give a little bit. We decided we liked peace better than winning."

I thought about that after my friend left. There is a profound truth there. Sometimes we just have to lay down our weapons. We have to let our agendas go. We have to be willing to sacrifice our own way to the way of the relationship. A harmonious relationship takes two people who both wish to lay down their arms, to call a truce. If only one surrenders and the other continues to fire away, a marriage will still get destroyed.

Our weapons can destroy harmony in a marriage. What are those weapons?

The weapon of words. Like stealth bombers, words can sneak in and hit the target almost before the other person knows what happened. Like launched missiles, words cannot be retrieved. So we throw word-grenades back and forth, disrupting harmony and our marriage in the process.

The weapon of keeping score. Keeping score doesn't allow for forgiveness. Grace just seems to be too big a gift to give our spouse who may have betrayed us at some point. And when we are angry or hurt, we dredge up the past and fire it point-blank at our spouse, reminding him or her that we can never forget the wrongs against us.

The weapon of jealousy. When our jealousy causes us to question the company our spouse keeps and the activities our spouse engages in, we demonstrate again and again that we do not trust him or her. The insecurity caused by our jealousy compels us to monitor our spouse to prevent him or her from unfairly comparing us to other people. As a result, our spouse must tiptoe through a field of land mines to avoid angering or upsetting us.

Unless we disarm ourselves and agree not to use these threatening weapons, we can never have true harmony. Harmony is different from a truce. Some marriages declare a truce, but the individuals are still armed to the teeth.

What promotes harmony?

Harmony requires us to disarm. Disarmament means to lay down our defense mechanisms. Jesus said, "Blessed are the peacemakers" (Matt. 5:9, NKJV). To disarm is not to bury our head in the sand, never to confront again. Disarming means we confront in a way that does not diminish the other person. It means we show respect and love while agreeing to disagree.

Harmony gives up the right to win. But conflict must be resolved with harmony in mind. It often takes a conscious effort to remind ourselves that winning is not the goal. In fact,

sometimes we may win the battle but lose the war. My old college buddy demonstrated this insight in his own marriage.

Harmony involves praise. When you give praise to God and to your spouse, you set the table for harmony to come into your marriage. Praise defeats the spirit of guilt, condemnation, accusation, and argument. The prophet Isaiah admonishes us to put on "the garment of praise for the spirit of heaviness; that [we] might be called trees of righteousness, the planting of the Lord, that he might be glorified" (Isa. 61:3, KJV).

If your marriage is not at war, remember that it often does not take much to start one. Cherish your harmony by guarding the armory in your home. Stay disarmed. If you are at war in your marriage, remember that you and your spouse can begin the disarmament process today if you choose to do so.

Lord, disarm us by the power of Your Holy Spirit. Help us to guard the weapons in our arsenal, to be quick to surrender and slow to attack. Help us to cherish harmony more than winning. Amen.

REFLECTION

"By language, in all its facets, people live in peace or go to war. They sing hymns in harmony or shout insults. They express love or hatred. Within the intimate world of marriage, language in all its facets is how couples live together in peace or pain."

Fred Kendall, Anna Kendall, and Mary Hollingsworth, *Speaking of Love*

"Romance thrives in beautiful, quiet settings like the garden, where there is time to enjoy one another away from everyday distractions. . . . Talking quietly, breathing in the achingly beautiful fragrance of the earth . . . the excitement of being near one another mingles with the comfort of feeling safe and cherished."

Emilie Barnes, quoted in *Quiet Moments for Couples*

LET'S TALK ABOUT IT

1. What repeated arguments erode harmony in your marriage? What can you do to change this pattern?

2. What are the weapons you and your spouse are prone to use the most? What can you do to disarm?

YOUR NOTES/REFLECTIONS/PRAYERS/GOALS

_____

_____

_____

_____

_____

_____

_____

_____

_____

_____

_____

_____

Harmony

PRAYING FOR THE PRESENCE OF GOD IN OUR

GOOD HUMOR

42 . . . .

You will go out in joy and be led forth in peace; the mountains and hills will burst

into song before you, and all the trees of the field will clap their hands.

Isaiah 55:12, NIV

PRAYER

Lord, You created us with "funny bones." You are the author of joy and humor and laughter. We embrace this sense of well-being in our marriage and in our hearts. Help us to be able to laugh at ourselves and laugh with others. Help us to not take life so seriously that we fail to see the humor all about us. In Jesus' name, amen.

SCRIPTURE

"Sarah said, 'God has brought me laughter, and everyone who hears about this will laugh with me'"
(Gen. 21:6, NIV).

Humor is a wonderful thing—even when it comes during prayer time. A couple of Sundays ago, our family was praying together before we all left for separate destinations. Our daughter, Amy, was getting ready to go on a music tour to California, and her cat, Spooky, was very sick. We were all distressed over it, especially Amy. Spooky was like a member of the family. So when it was my turn to pray, I began to pray for Spooky, "Lord, You said that You cared about the birds that fall, so surely You care about Spooky." Suddenly, everyone began to giggle. It seemed to hit all of us at once, and soon we were practically rolling on the floor in laughter—in the middle of this prayer. You see, Spooky has killed more than his share of birds, and it suddenly seemed very funny to be reminding God that He cares about birds in the same breath that I was asking God to save Spooky's life. We all ended up in hilarious laughter during that prayer. Later we cried, too, when Spooky died. We loved that old cat.

I know that God was not displeased with the humor of that moment. The thing is, God cares about the most intimate details of our lives. There is no division between sacred and secular. What do we think? That God tunes in to us only when we have long, somber expressions on our faces and use a stained-glass voice? No! We listen to our children when they cry, but we also love it when they laugh. God does too.

Martin Luther once said, "If you're not allowed to laugh in heaven, I don't want to go there." Jesus told us He came "so that my joy may be in you" (John 15:11, NIV). And then Jesus punctuates this by declaring, "Yes, your cup of joy will overflow!" (John 15:11, TLB). It is a wonderful experience to laugh. That is why we will go out of our way to listen to a good comedian. We all like the experience of laughter. God would not have created us with that emotion if He did not expect us to enjoy it.

Medical science is now beginning to discover what a very wise man knew several thousand years ago. King Solomon said, "A merry heart does good, like medicine" (Prov. 17:22, NKJV). Humor can be a powerful tool toward healing. In her article "Go Ahead . . . Laugh," Nancy Kennedy reports on a study done by William Fry, a psychiatrist, laugh researcher, and professor emeritus at Stanford University Medical School. Fry says that deep belly laughs benefit the entire body because the entire physiology of the person laughing is involved. A hearty laugh also gives the heart a cardiovascular workout and massages the muscles in the face, diaphragm, and abdomen. The psychiatrist says that laughing also lowers blood pressure. Evidently, it is indeed good medicine to laugh.

Good Humor

There are, however, good ways and bad ways to use humor in marriage. When the joke or humor is at the expense of our spouse, it is usually bad humor. The reason is because in a casual way we may be diminishing our spouse. Jokes or funny stories at the expense of someone else are usually uncomfortable for the person who becomes the brunt of the joke. If you want to tell a funny story, tell one on yourself, not on your spouse. Laughing at our own mistakes or seeing humor in our circumstances is a better use of humor. Seeing the funny side of what otherwise could be a tense situation can also be a good use of humor.

You can assist each other in finding good humor. Look for humor in everyday situations, and then tell the story to your spouse. Read funny books to each other. Give each other crazy greeting cards. Sometimes, when Bill and I need a good laugh, we will purposely go visit the local greeting-card shop and read each other funny birthday or anniversary cards. Now the owner has gotten used to hearing our belly laughs from over in the corner. Sometimes she starts laughing just listening to us.

Laughter is contagious. If laughter is also healthy, as Dr. Fry says, and if it is spiritual, as the Bible indicates, then you should go out of your way to make each other laugh.

Lord, we want our marriage to be filled with healthy laughter. Help us to be a couple with good humor exuding from our house. Help us to be quick to see the light side of life. When we experience stress, help us to be able to say, "Someday we'll laugh at this," and then help us to go ahead and laugh! Amen.

Good Humor

REFLECTION

"Two researchers at the Yale School of Medicine, Dr. Frederick C. Redlich and Professor Jacob Levine, found that an inability to appreciate humor can indicate emotional problems. Usually a person with a well-developed sense of humor has a well-developed personality. In contrast, those who rarely see humor in a joke or cartoon often are emotionally maladjusted, the researchers concluded. Their inability to release tension in socially appropriate ways, such as through laughter, could be either a cause of or a result of their emotional disorders."

Rusty Wright and Linda Raney Wright, *Secrets of Successful Humor*

"Humor is a prelude to faith, and laughter is the beginning of prayer."

Reinhold Niebuhr, quoted in *"Go Ahead . . . Laugh"*

1 Are you and your spouse able to laugh at life's circumstances at times? Can you sometimes find humor even in stressful situations? Can you laugh at yourself?

2 What do you do to create opportunity for humor in your marriage?

YOUR NOTES/REFLECTIONS/PRAYERS/GOALS

Good Humor

PART 8

Values

True Love

Wisdom

Fruit of the Spirit

Letting Go

Learning

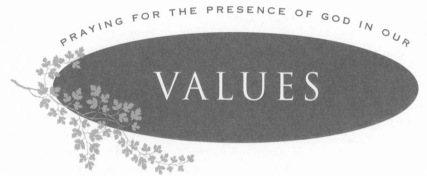

PRAYING FOR THE PRESENCE OF GOD IN OUR

VALUES

43 . . . .

Oh, the joys of those who do not follow the advice of the wicked,

or stand around with sinners, or join in with scoffers. But they delight in doing

everything the Lord wants; day and night they think about his law. They are like

trees planted along the riverbank, bearing fruit each season without fail.

Their leaves never wither, and in all they do, they prosper.

Psalm 1:1-3

PRAYER

Lord, may we do the right thing individually and as a couple, even when it costs us. Help us to see others as Your precious creations and to treat them with respect, withholding judgment, knowing You are fair and righteous. Give us grace, understanding, and justice, helping us to extend them to one another and to those around us. Give us courage to stand for truth and righteousness not only in our own marriage but also in the world. May we not compromise what is right, regardless of what it costs us. Amen.

"Store your treasures in heaven. . . . Wherever your treasure is, there your heart and thoughts will also be" *(Matt. 6:20-21).*

Marriage is mysterious, complex; we are individuals, yet a team. We can be so close that sometimes we don't know where one person leaves off and the other begins. Yet in some ways we are so utterly opposite from each other that we seem to be from different planets. How do we forge a set of values that works for us as individuals and as a couple?

What would you say your values are now? Do you value privacy? Is financial success important to you? Do you prize community involvement? Do you value church commitment and personal spiritual growth?

Be intentional about your values. Talk together about them. Don't assume that you know what your spouse's values are on certain matters. We all come from different places in life. We all face the pressures of our cultural values.

Our values are reflected in the myriad of choices and decisions that we make every day. We express what we value in how we spend our time and money, in our dreams and goals. What we treasure—what is closest to our hearts—becomes what we value. It is what we protect above all else. It is what we must have at all costs.

When you look at the values your marriage reflects, do you like what you see? How can we shape godly values in our marriage?

We must value choosing God's ways. Having godly values means recognizing that there is a right way and a wrong way. It means saying no to certain things and yes to others. It may mean self-sacrifice. Choosing God's way often means going against the tide, giving up our desire to please ourselves at all costs. It means resisting temptation if it takes us away from what is right. Sarah and Ben were on vacation with two other couples in the city. All three couples were Christians, but Sarah and Ben faced a dilemma when their friends wanted to go to a pornographic movie. Sarah and Ben declined, but they endured teasing from their friends for being "frigid" and "legalistic." Years later, Sarah and Ben told us they still feel good about that decision, even at the risk of looking like "Goody Two-shoes." Being moral may not always make you popular, but it will take you in the right direction to establish strong values that will protect your marriage through the years.

We must value our marriage vows. Shauna told us that a defining moment in her life came

Values

when she recognized she was playing around with something dangerous . . . a past relationship that she justified as just a good friendship. She said, "I repented and realized I had to let go of the past. I burned old pictures and letters. That past relationship was keeping my marriage in bondage. When I took that step, it was amazing how my marriage improved." The New Testament says it like this: "Surrender to God! Resist the devil, and he will run from you. Come near to God, and he will come near to you. Clean up your lives. . . . Purify your hearts" (James 4:7-8, CEV). When we face the inevitable temptations, it is no time to be heroic. It's time to get out of the tempting situation. *Leave.*

We must value what is right over what is convenient. An important value is to do what's right in spite of personal cost, to live with integrity. We must ask, Where are our affections? Some of the best, most worthy treasures are hidden, and we must seek them out. We will live with an inner sense of peace and joy if we are honest with each other, if we stay pure in our actions as well as in our thoughts, and if we live out our commitment in spite of the temptations. It is crucial to decide what values we will live by before we face moments of temptation. When we pre-determine to be committed to God's values, our chances of making the right decision in the heat of the battle are much improved. The Word of God warns us, "Be careful. If you are thinking, 'Oh, I would never behave like that'—let this be a warning to you. For you too may fall into sin" (1 Cor. 10:12, TLB).

God, our hearts cry out for You! How we need Your presence in our lives, in our marriage. Forgive us for having so many other things that crowd out the important values. Give us the courage to define our values according to your guidelines and then to live by them, whatever the cost. Lord, come into our marriage, be Lord of our marriage. We want to value You and Your ways above all else in life. Give us the courage to seek guidance from Your Word so that we may walk this life together, seeking after righteousness. Amen.

REFLECTION

"The divine Presence does not come as a courteous guest. He makes demands.
He goes through every room, looks under the rugs, opens drawers. Up to the attic, down to the
basement, into all the closets and storage places. Everywhere he wants to know, 'What's this?
What's that?' And if we let him stay, some things will have to go, some changes will need to be made.
Changes in ourselves, changes in attitudes, changes in our relationship to each other. . . .
For the Christian couple, marriage means the Lord is shaping this relationship to his design."

Charlie and Martha Shedd, "Praying Together"

"Image is what people think we are. Integrity is what we really are."

John Maxwell, *Developing the Leader within You*

LET'S TALK ABOUT IT

1 Discuss with your spouse what your values are. How have you formed your values, and what feeds them?

2 List ten values that you both agree are most important to you as a couple. How can you protect these values?

YOUR NOTES/REFLECTIONS/PRAYERS/GOALS

_____

_____

_____

_____

_____

_____

_____

_____

_____

_____

_____

Values

TRUE LOVE

44

The greatest love is shown when people lay down their lives for their friends.

John 15:12-13

PRAYER

Lord, I recognize that my marriage is a precious gift from You. Just as You have given my spouse to me as a gift, I am called to give my spouse my best—my love, my devotion, my help, my protection, my loyalty, and my never-ending belief in his or her calling and giftedness. Help me give these things fully and joyfully as an act of true love. In Jesus' name, amen.

SCRIPTURE

"Live a life filled with love for others, following the example of Christ, who loved you and gave himself as a sacrifice to take away your sins" (Eph. 5:1-2).

As Nancie and I look back over our marriage, it seems to us now that the challenge of loving each other is not so much in *doing* as in *being*. We want to be loving people. It sounds so simple, yet it's so hard. After thirty-plus years of marriage we are just now catching glimpses of what it means to truly love each other. It is indeed wonderful to feel loved. Victor Hugo wrote, "The supreme happiness of life is the conviction that we are loved." And yet love begets love. True love—the servant-spirit kind of love that Jesus demonstrates—takes us beyond trying to get the love we need to *giving* that kind of unconditional love with no strings attached. It means living the principle found in Scripture: "Give, and it will be given to you" (Luke 6:38, NIV).

True Love

What does true love look like? True love is difficult to describe, and yet we recognize it. In his book *Seeds of Hope,* Henri Nouwen described marriage as "a relationship in which a man and a woman protect and nurture the inner sanctum within and between them and witness to that by the way they love each other. . . . Marriage . . . is an intimacy based on the common participation in a love greater than the love two people can offer each other. They are brought together, indeed, as two prayerful hands extended toward God and forming in this way a home for God in this world." True love is greater than we are.

The English language has only one word for *love,* and we use it liberally to describe a variety of emotions and behaviors. Some languages have more words to describe love. Love can be a deep friendship. Love can be a romantic relationship. "Making love" refers to sexual intercourse. "Tough love" refers to loving someone enough to confront. "Enduring love" is an I-will-be-with-you-no-matter-what love.

A good marriage involves all of these loves as well as a love that says, "I am dedicated to your growth as a person. I am committed to your joy. I am here to serve you. I am willing to forgive you for being imperfect." This is not easy. It requires sacrifice, trust, commitment, grace, and forgiveness. It often requires postponement of one's own gratification.

Married love is hard work because it requires us to think first of our spouse instead of ourselves. Many marriage ceremonies contain the words of Paul: "Husbands must love your wives with the same love Christ showed the church. He gave up his life for her" (Eph. 5:25). I think the second part of those instructions is actually easier than the first. I think that if my wife were somehow threatened, I could do the necessary thing to protect her, even if it meant I would lose my life. But to *live* for my wife means to put her first over my own self, to be committed to her growth, to try to meet her needs, to lovingly confront her, to challenge her to be all God intends her to be, to see her reach her potential, to be her friend, confidant, and ally.

I often fail at this because of my own needs and wants. But the beauty is that when two people are committed to each other in this way, the failures are accepted as part of the process, and the relationship still grows.

True love involves grace. Grace is a powerful ingredient in marriage. It involves forgiving and forgetting. It means we don't keep score. It means we give a second chance to the ones we love when they make mistakes. None of us has reached this perfect stage of love, but if you have a partner who is committed to this kind of true love, you are indeed blessed. If you do not, it can begin with you.

The need to be loved is a primal one. We do enormous things to make love happen. We desperately seek to marry the right person. We work incredibly hard to be accepted, liked, loved. We go to seminars and read books about how we can love. But love cannot be forced. It is like the blossoming of a beautiful flower. God plants the seed of love, then encourages us to learn from Him. And it is in the learning that it happens. When we get caught up in the doing, we expect payment for services rendered: "You owe me." The bottom line is that we can love each other because Jesus first loved us. To experience and live that love is a lifetime journey.

Lord, come into our marriage. Entirely. May we live the metaphor of Your love. We humbly and brokenly offer ourselves to You. Teach us the lessons, the intricacies of love. Teach us grace. Teach us to experience it and to offer it to one another. Forgive us for not letting go of past anger, past injustice, and unrealized expectations. Help us to grow up in You, Lord, and truly know what it means to love. Amen.

REFLECTION

"Love seeks one thing only: the good of the one loved. It leaves all other secondary effects to take care of themselves. Love, therefore, is its own reward."

Thomas Merton, quoted in *Quiet Moments for Couples*

"And so it is in marriage that when the Lord draws a man and a woman together in the most intimate of human associations, He does so by giving them His love, which is the only thing that can shield them through the searing experience of self-revelation they are to undergo. This is an experience that all people both crave and fear, with a fear that is conquerable only by love. Only love can drive out the constant threat of condemnation and rejection that otherwise haunts and spoils all experiences of intimacy."

Mike Mason, *The Mystery of Marriage*

1   Over a period of time (one week is good), read 1 Corinthians 13 together. Keep notes about what you are learning about love. Pray for insights to impact your marriage with what it means to truly love.

2   At the end of the one-week period, set aside time for talking about how you were able to display love to one another in practical ways. What area needs improvement?

YOUR NOTES/REFLECTIONS/PRAYERS/GOALS

_____

_____

_____

_____

_____

_____

_____

_____

_____

_____

_____

_____

_____

True Love

PRAYING FOR THE PRESENCE OF GOD IN OUR

WISDOM

45

How much better to get wisdom than gold, and understanding than silver!

Proverbs 16:16

PRAYER

Lord, we want to live lives of wisdom. We know that knowing You is the first step toward wisdom, and we come to You, asking for Your wisdom. Life is too complicated if we do not rest fully on You. Teach us Your ways, O Lord, and may we seek out Your wisdom as the ultimate treasure in life. In Jesus' name, amen.

SCRIPTURE

"Getting wisdom is the most important thing you can do! And whatever else you do, get good judgment" (Prov. 4:7).

Dorothy and Earl Book, whom we regard as our spiritual and marriage mentors, personify wisdom to us. Now in their seventies, they are still active in ministry, still growing in wisdom. Bible study and prayer together begin their day, and you can see in their life pursuits how much they both love God and people. Seeking God's wisdom first has been their life investment, and it is paying off richly.

Nancie and I also highly respect my parents as people filled with wisdom. They just celebrated sixty years of marriage together and are still vitally involved in the lives of their children, their friends, and their church. They actively seek the Lord first for His guidance. When we think of wisdom, often we think of someone older, people seasoned through time. But it's possible to be young and growing in wisdom, too—and it's also possible to be older and unwise.

What does wisdom look like in marriage? How can we develop it?

Wisdom in marriage acknowledges God's wisdom. A couple who develops wisdom first of all realizes the *source* of all wisdom—the Lord. The writer of Proverbs reminds us, "Fear of the Lord is the beginning of wisdom" (Prov. 9:10). As I mentioned earlier, the Books and my parents consciously seek God's wisdom through their Bible study and prayer. We admire that about them and want to emulate that in our marriage.

Wisdom in marriage comes through listening. Wisdom also grows through a listening attitude: "Listen to counsel and receive instruction, that you may be wise in your latter days" (Prov. 19:20, NKJV). Nancie and I have grown so much through the advice and instruction of other people. If we had started out our marriage convinced that we had all the answers, we would have failed. But along the way couples have shared with us their failures and victories, and we have learned from them how to avoid mistakes and how to make better decisions.

Wisdom in marriage involves doing what is right. Sometimes we think that wisdom is an abstract, illusive idea. Basically, wisdom is knowing what's right and doing it. That's certainly a concrete idea and a good place to start our quest to be wise. Scripture reminds us, "We end our lives with a groan. . . . But even the best of these years are filled with pain and trouble; soon they disappear, and we are gone. . . . Teach us to make the most of our time, so that we may grow in wisdom" (Ps. 90:9-12). Wisdom means understanding now what is true, right, and lasting.

Wisdom in marriage commits to growth. Change is inevitable. People are not static, and neither are relationships. Growth means that we embrace the changes and view them as stepping-stones to becoming better people, to becoming people of wisdom. It means we stay flexible enough to see our marriage change as we change.

It is immature to think that the person I married more than thirty years ago when she was eighteen is the same person now. It is unfair for me to hold her to some youthful expectation I may have had about our relationship. We both have made significant changes physically, emotionally, spiritually, and vocationally. We are different people. Life has developed us, shaped us, molded us.

Nancie and I have found that as we commit ourselves to growth, both as individuals and as a couple, we have been able to weather the storms of change. At times we have grown because of each other's resistance to change. At times we have grown together through hardship or adversity. Sometimes we have experienced failure or loss together. At times one of us has grown in an area that the other did not experience until later. Those times required patience and understanding.

Wisdom in marriage takes time. Becoming people of wisdom takes time. It's a process of testing, waiting, studying, and listening. It is a process of learning as we go through life. Ted and Cherry made these comments about wisdom in their marriage: "Sometimes we look back on the early years of our marriage and are embarrassed by some of the decisions we made, decisions we thought were wise at the time. But we value those memories because they are part of the learning process. We don't pretend to be the epitome of wisdom now, after fifteen years of marriage, but we are maturing as we continue to ask for God's guidance, as we listen to people who are more wise than we are, and as we learn from our mistakes."

Lord, may we recognize You first of all as the true, ultimate source of wisdom. May we always go to You first, seek Your guidance first, trust Your Word first in our lives together as a couple. We pray that we will be committed to grow in wisdom through whatever life brings us, knowing we are safe in Your care. Amen.

REFLECTION

"Welcome change as a friend; try to visualize new possibilities and the blessings it is bound to bring you. If you stay interested in everything around you—in new ways of life, new people, new places and ideas—you'll stay young, no matter what your age. Never stop learning and never stop growing; that is the key to a rich and fascinating life."

Alexander DeSeversky, quoted in *How to Change Your Spouse*

"To journey for the sake of saving our own lives is little by little to cease to live in any sense that really matters, even to ourselves, because it is only by journeying for the world's sake—even when the world bores and sickens and scares you half to death—that little by little we start to come alive."

Frederick Buechner, *The Sacred Journey*

LET'S TALK ABOUT IT

1. Prayerfully consider your marriage now. What can you do to move along the path toward wisdom?

2. What are practical things that both of you can do to acknowledge God first, seek Him first?

YOUR NOTES/REFLECTIONS/PRAYERS/GOALS

_____

_____

_____

_____

_____

_____

_____

_____

_____

_____

_____

Wisdom

FRUIT
OF THE SPIRIT

46

But when the Holy Spirit controls our lives, he will produce

this kind of fruit in us: love, joy, peace, patience, kindness, goodness,

faithfulness, gentleness, and self-control.

Galatians 5:22-23

PRAYER

Lord, how we need the fruit of Your Spirit. We live in a fast-paced culture that does not encourage patience or kindness or self-control. Yet our marriage needs those qualities. Teach us to be loving and joyful and gentle—all of the wonderful qualities that reflect You. Lord, we know it is in the everyday challenges of life that we learn these things. Thank You for the opportunity to grow in these areas. In Jesus' name, amen.

"Since God chose you to be the holy people whom he loves, you must clothe yourselves with tenderhearted mercy, kindness, humility, gentleness, and patience. And the most important piece of clothing you must wear is love" (Col. 3:12, 14).

INSIGHT

It is not easy to get ready for a vacation. Especially when you try to sandwich it right after a speaking engagement, a bookseller's conference, and a month of organizing children's summer jobs. The idea was to take time to get away, but by the time Bill and I got on our boat with all the supplies we thought we would need for the week, I was beginning to wonder if it was worth it. Let's just say that the fruit of the Spirit was in short supply.

Bill, Andy, Amy, and I decided to sleep in the boat tied up at the dock that night since it was so late. We awoke early the next morning to find nearly a foot of water on the floor, within six inches of our kids' sleeping bags. We began pumping water as fast as we could. We realized we had to take the boat out of the water to find the problem. As I stood on the dock watching our little red boat being hauled out after all we had gone through to get there, I wondered what else could go wrong. But more than the obvious problem of fixing our boat was the underlying tension between Bill and me. We were out of sorts. The last thing I wanted to do was be on a small boat with four crabby people, one of them, admittedly, me.

As I sat waiting for the mechanic and Bill to come back to fix the boat, I dug out my Bible. My Scripture reading for the day was John 2, which tells the story of Jesus at a marriage feast where the hosts ran out of wine. Jesus' mother told the servants, "Do whatever he tells you" (John 2:5). Jesus told the servants to fill the waterpots with water and then to pour some out and serve it. You know the story. The water became wine, better even than the wine served earlier at the feast. It was a miracle. As I sat and thought about that story, somehow it seemed applicable to what was going on between Bill and me and our disrupted plans.

I sat on the dock in my jeans and sweatshirt and prayed, *Lord, somehow I've run out of the wine of joy in my marriage lately. Would you please come into our marriage? Show us how to have the fruit of the Spirit in our lives.* It was a simple prayer, but I have never forgotten it because Jesus did show up. And it seemed to me that He was saying to me, "Just pour it out. In the midst of the ordinary day, the frustrations, live the fruit of the Spirit. Do it not because you feel like it or because it's spontaneous. Do it because you are Mine and because you choose to obey Me." In other words, He said to me, pour out love, pour out gentleness, pour out patience, pour out joy. Something wonderful happened. Obeying Jesus (even if I didn't feel like it) brought love, gentleness, patience, joy. Soon the leak in our boat was fixed, and we were on our way. I never forgot that morning, though, because I learned in a simple but memorable way what it means to walk in the Spirit.

We can have the fruit of the Spirit even in very difficult situations, not just in ordinary things. One couple went through the crushing experience of mutual infidelity, something that would destroy most marriages. Tom and Rhonda told us, "Our marriage survived because we decided to forgive what neither of us found forgivable. God's Spirit gave us the ability to break through the anger, fear, and hopelessness with patience and goodness and self-control—qualities we knew were not our own. Love and good feelings have been restored, along with hope and vision." God's grace is great, and the fruit of the Spirit becomes evident in our lives when we come to Him in humility.

We must be patient with one another, allowing God to deal with our spouse. As we give patience and understanding, it is amazing what can happen in a relationship. In *Till the Heart Be Touched,* Gail and Gordon MacDonald wrote, "Simply put, patience is the willingness to generously give another person time and space to grow. Patience means we downsize our expectations, our timetables, our methods, and permit God's purposes to prevail. Patience does not demand; it lovingly waits."

Lord, help us to remember that life doesn't just have to happen to us. We can choose to obey You. We can choose attitudes that reflect You, and we can avoid being controlled by our lower natures. May we be willing to be Your servants and obey You even if we don't feel like it, even if it seems illogical, knowing that You can do miracles with what we give You—especially our attitudes! In Jesus' name, amen.

Fruit of the Spirit

REFLECTION

*"I love you because you are helping me to make
Of the lumber of my life
Not a tavern, but a temple;
Out of the words of my everyday
Not a reproach, but a song."*

Joan Winmill Brown and Bill Brown, *Together Each Day*

"You will find, as you look back upon your life, that the moments that stand out, the moments when you have really lived, are the moments when you have done things in the spirit of Love."

Henry Drummond, quoted in *Quiet Moments for Couples*

LET'S TALK ABOUT IT

1. Read Galatians 5 together and discuss how you see the fruit of the Spirit—love, joy, peace, patience, kindness, goodness, faithfulness, gentleness, and self-control—in your spouse.

2. Share with one another what areas you believe you would most like to develop more. (Avoid pointing out the other's area—let God do that!)

YOUR NOTES/REFLECTIONS/PRAYERS/GOALS

_____

_____

_____

_____

_____

_____

_____

_____

_____

_____

_____

Fruit of the Spirit

LETTING GO

47

There is no fear in love; but perfect love casts out fear, because fear involves torment.

But he who fears has not been made perfect in love.

1 John 4:18, NKJV

PRAYER

Lord, help us to understand that it is in giving that we truly receive and that when we hold on too tightly, we destroy. We know that it is harmful to our marriage to be excessively possessive. Teach us to give each other room to grow and develop into all that You have gifted us to be. Help us realize that as we let go of controlling behavior, our love for each other will not diminish but grow stronger than ever. Amen.

SCRIPTURE

"We know what real love is because Christ gave up his life for us. And so we also ought to give up our lives for our Christian brothers and sisters" (1 John 3:16).

Lisa and Jeff loved each other *so much* that they could hardly let each other get out of sight. They bumped their engagement up early so they could marry as soon as possible. They *needed* each other. As time went on in their marriage, they were blessed with two little boys who kept Lisa busy and fulfilled. True to his gregarious nature, Jeff got involved as a local school board member. That meant lots of meetings, but Jeff enjoyed it. He was also running a family-owned business that was rapidly growing and required a lot of his attention. Lisa, an introvert, didn't want to be involved with the school or the business. She was grateful that she didn't have to work out of the home so she could be with her young sons, but she was not happy with Jeff. She told us, "I grew to hate everything he did."

She felt that he was pulling away from her and that he didn't need her anymore. On the other hand, she needed him—a lot—but the more she tried to tell him, the more he withdrew. And it didn't help their time together because Lisa was so filled with resentment toward Jeff when they were together that it seemed better just to let things slide.

This went on for a rather miserable seventeen years. It is a wonder their marriage survived, but they hung in there because they both were committed to God and to raising their children together. Then a change began when Lisa decided not to begrudge Jeff his involvements and to take some responsibility for her happiness instead of waiting for Jeff to make her happy. She enrolled in some night classes at the local college. She had always wanted to finish her degree, and Jeff actively encouraged her. She began to develop a new level of self-confidence. At first Jeff was almost insecure because he was married to a "new Lisa." But as time went on, they both grew, and their marriage is much more balanced now as Lisa has grown to let go of her demands on Jeff. The interesting thing is that as she grew more independent, Jeff wanted to be with her more.

How can we let go in a healthy way in our marriage? First of all, remember that your marriage is unique to you. There are no set rules on what a husband should do or a wife should do; that is something both of you must decide. Demanding time together is not letting go. Ignoring your obvious problems and escaping by doing your own thing is not letting go.

Letting go means releasing your spouse. True love lets go. In a healthy way, true love releases our spouse to be all that God wants for him or her. At first letting go seems to be the opposite of love; love seems to want to possess one another. But when we can't let go, we are really saying that we can't exist without the other person. That is a heavy burden to put on anybody; it's like having a leech or a parasite on our body. There are times we like to feel "that needed," but over time, it can be suffocating.

Letting go means leaving space in your togetherness. A poet once wrote that we need "space in our togetherness." Space means respecting the other person as a whole person, not just as someone who keeps you alive. I learned that it's quite all right for Bill to go on a fishing trip with the guys and for me to go shopping with my sisters. Often both Bill and I are happier for it. Bill will never understand how shopping can be fun, and I fail to understand how getting up at four in the morning to be cold and miserable for one scraggly fish can be fun. We have agreed to have space in our togetherness for certain things.

Letting go means giving to your spouse. We can truly give to one another when we have taken responsibility for ourselves and our happiness. When Lisa was able to let go of demanding that Jeff make her happy, she found that she was also able to let go of her resentment. That freed her to give to Jeff in healthy ways. She became more tolerant, understanding, giving.

Lord, I pray that I will see my spouse as You do—a unique, wonderful person with gifts and talents that can be developed to their fullest potential. I pray that my letting-go love will let my beloved one soar. Teach us to love one another with respect, without fear of losing one another. In Jesus' name, amen.

REFLECTION

"Marriage is the soil for growing glory. We must see our spouses in light of what they are meant to become, without turning bitter or complacent about who they are. Marriage requires a radical commitment to love our spouses as they are, while longing for them to become what they are not yet. Every marriage moves either toward enhancing one another's glory or toward degrading each other."

Dan B. Allender and Tremper Longman III, *Intimate Allies*

"Keeping kills. Relinquishing heals. . . . We do not quickly divest ourselves. But the question will have been put. . . . An invitation will have been issued. Return to the command, to the God who rests and gives rest, who sets free and satisfies. . . . We do not yield easily. But . . . if we do not yield, we shall die."

Walter Brueggemann, *Finally Comes the Poet*

LET'S TALK ABOUT IT

1 In what areas of your relationship might you be holding on too closely? Discuss the difference between being fair to one another and letting go.

2 How can you give each other more space and yet increase intimacy?

YOUR NOTES/REFLECTIONS/PRAYERS/GOALS

Letting Go

PRAYING FOR THE PRESENCE OF GOD IN OUR

LEARNING

48

Let the wise listen and add to their learning, and let the discerning get guidance.

Proverbs 1:5, NIV

PRAYER

O God, as we change and grow, help us grow toward You. Let us never envy others whose situation may seem better or easier or more fruitful than ours is. Let us be faithful where You have us. May we put our roots down deep so that we will grow from where we are. Thank You for Your faithfulness. Amen.

SCRIPTURE

"Blessed is the man whose strength is in You, whose heart is set on pilgrimage" (Ps. 84:5, NKJV).

It was a beautiful day in the Colorado mountains when our friends Gene and Marylou went hiking with several other people. After a mile or so, it became apparent that the group was splitting up into two groups: one group pressed on at full speed, and the other group ambled more slowly. Gene and Marylou stayed in the second group, enjoying the scenery and keeping pace with those who didn't want to go at a breakneck speed in the high altitude. "That day pointed out something important to us about marriage," Gene remembered. "Life is like a journey, and in a marriage, two people start out on the path together. Sometimes one of them will take off ahead, and if they aren't careful, they can get separated on the journey."

If *both* the husband and wife do not keep growing, they can become separated by their life's experience. Remember: Learning keeps you young, and it keeps life interesting as you stay involved and growing.

Learning begins with me. When I was a young woman, I made a promise to myself one day in my kitchen: "Whatever happens in my life, I promise that I will keep growing, that I will never stop learning as long as I live." I said it simply, almost as a prayer, but I have never forgotten that moment. The choice to learn was one of the most important decisions I ever made, and I've had lots of opportunities to put that choice into action. Our lives offer many places to go on to the next step, to grow. Sometimes we miss them, but God is faithful and gives us other times. He speaks to us often through the uncomfortable places: our fears and insecurities and pain. I personally have learned the most eloquently through my weaknesses and struggles. It's a good thing I made that promise because Bill is happiest when he is learning something new. Keeping up with him has been a challenge. Often I'm just getting up to speed on something, and he's way ahead on the next thing. But I have enjoyed the challenge.

Learning also begins with God. When the hunger to learn and know and grow is under the umbrella of God's wisdom, learning is a wonderful thing. How do we learn about God? By studying His Word, trusting Him, trying Him. The more we trust Him, the more we will learn of Him as we go. Real maturity often means letting go more and more to follow Him. It's not so much that we "have more of Jesus" but that He "has more of us." More of our thoughts, our dreams, our ambitions, our wants.

As we pray together, we learn more about God and more about our walk with Him. In His presence is the common ground where we can begin to learn the most important things ever. Our Lord invites us: "Call to Me, and I will answer you, and show you great and mighty things, which you do not know" (Jer. 33:3, NKJV).

Learning involves helping each other. We can encourage one another in our learning of God. Even though Bill and I both love God and are committed to His ways, the goal of pursuing Him has at times been murky, not always in sync. We've learned it helps to keep pace together by sharing the same experiences. If at all possible, attend an inspirational retreat together or listen to some challenging tapes as you drive in the car and talk about your responses. Bill has encouraged me to read some of the historical writings he is excited about; I share with him some theological nuggets I find. If possible, commit to going to at least one couples' class or small group together during the year. Grow *together.*

Learning includes risk. Let's face it, all of us are continuing to learn in this school of marriage, and some of the stages and phases are more difficult than others, depending on many factors. We can continue to grow in knowledge, improving our understanding of each other, keeping an ongoing education as a couple and individually. When Bill and I first started out as a young couple, we thought that the challenges we had to overcome to have a successful life would be things like getting an education and good jobs. What we did not see then was that the real challenges to growth were not as obvious but every bit as intimidating. They are the things that lie inside of us: insecurities, our need for approval, negative attitudes, self-centeredness, pride, and low self-esteem. But growth inevitably involves risk, and growth often comes in the moments we would most like to avoid—usually in the places of our weaknesses and fears.

Learning never stops. Stay on the path of new discovery together, and your life as a couple will be much richer.

Lord, thank You for the richness of life's experiences. We pray that we will be hungry to learn more about life, about how we can grow in You. Keep us learning, inspiring each other to stretch and grow. Amen.

REFLECTION

"A difficulty in a marriage could be a sign that it's time to start growing. People don't want to accept negatives. They think negatives mean, 'It's over; I have to leave,' rather than try and work through the problem."

Natalie Robins, *The Heart of Marriage*

"The book of Proverbs says, 'As iron sharpens iron, so one person sharpens another.' Our incompleteness and differences give iron its roughness, its sharpening power. Marriage is a God-given way to improve and hone our beings. Marriage challenges us to new heights and calls us to be the best person possible, but neither marriage nor our partner will magically make us whole."

Les and Leslie Parrott, *Saving Your Marriage Before It Starts*

LET'S TALK ABOUT IT

1 How have both of you grown since you were first married? In what areas of your life have you learned the most?

2 In what area is your learning lopsided, with one of you ahead on the path? How can you be more together in this area?

YOUR NOTES/REFLECTIONS/PRAYERS/GOALS

_____

_____

_____

_____

_____

_____

_____

_____

_____

_____

Learning

Losses

Stress

Valley Times

Seasons

PART *9*

PRAYING FOR THE PRESENCE OF GOD IN OUR

LOSSES

49

Even though I walk through the valley of the shadow of death, I will fear no evil,

for you are with me; your rod and your staff, they comfort me.

Psalm 23:4, NIV

PRAYER

How often, Lord, I don't fully comprehend real love. Help me to see that providing support is a vital part of my marriage. Lord, I ask for compassion, for that deep awareness and sensitivity to any suffering or losses my spouse may be experiencing. Give me the grace and strength to give comfort and support, even though I may not fully understand. In Jesus' name, amen.

SCRIPTURE

"For You are my safe refuge, a fortress where my enemies cannot reach me. Let me live forever in your sanctuary, safe beneath the shelter of your wings!" (Ps. 61: 3-4).

It has been said that God's greatest gifts to us often are disguised—wrapped in problems, trials, and sufferings. They are gifts because they often teach us important things that we would never learn otherwise.

Theresa shared her story with us. She told us that her first year of marriage to David was wonderful. But somehow, they got into a routine of taking each other for granted, and things began to grow cold between them. The relationship begin to spiral downward as arguments and accusations increased. "After thirteen years of misery I became pregnant with our third child," Theresa said. "At first, this put even more distance between us. While I was excited, David was very upset because it wasn't in his plans (he was forty-seven years old). But then, somehow, an amazing thing began to happen. The Lord began to soften both of our hearts through the little life growing in me, and David and I fell in love all over again."

It was shortly after this renewal of their marriage that tragedy struck. Here are Theresa's own words: "Unexpectedly, the Lord took our precious son home to be with Him. What a wake-up call. David and I realized that we had been wasting our lives with our self-centered needs, not seeing how precious life is. The next year was so incredible. We didn't have the strength to do anything without first going to the Lord. What an experience it is to totally rely on God and let Him

have full control of our marriage. It was hard to lose our new little love, but he will always be a special blessing because he taught his mommy and daddy how to love again."

It's impossible to know why some things happen. Jesus said, "In this world you will have trouble. But take heart! I have overcome the world" (John 16:33, NIV). Jesus didn't say, "In the off chance a storm will come" or "In the rare occurrence of a storm." Storms happen. Losses and disappointments are inevitable parts of life.

But it is important not to lose heart in our losses because it is often in the losses that He makes Himself real, that He refines us. We can respond to losses in two ways: We can become bitter and resentful, or we can let God's grace and compassion comfort and renew us. Someone has said that the same sun that softens wax, hardens clay. Our response to life's losses can turn us either way.

When we experience disappointment and loss, we often are left with lots of questions. We know that God answers prayer, yet at times He remains silent despite our most desperate pleas.

Years ago Bill and I were trying to buy a small house to use for a much-needed office. However, in the midst of our negotiations the zoning was changed. We earnestly prayed, convinced we were supposed to have that building, which seemed perfect for our

Losses

needs. Yet the harder we tried to complete the transaction, the more problems we encountered. We finally gave up on the building, full of questions. We had no idea then that a year later, a better building at a better price would become available. We could only look back with a sigh of relief and say, "Thank You, Lord!" Only God knows the future, and just because God doesn't give us the answer we are looking for doesn't mean He is ignoring our prayers.

Not long ago I listened to dear friends agonize over the fact that their son had just been served divorce papers. Their daughter-in-law said she had found someone better. My friend and her husband felt kicked in the stomach. I just listened to them, reminded again of our inability to understand some things. The questions rage: Why? What could have been said or done differently to prevent this?

A time of loss is a time to do four basic things. First, trust the Lord with all of your heart, even if you don't understand. Don't be afraid of what you perceive to be silence. Second, let the grieving happen. Give yourself space to let the emotions spill out. Find people who can hear your grief and help you process its various stages. Third, respect and tolerate your spouse's way of processing the loss. Remember that you will grieve in different ways and at a different pace. Finally, comfort each other, offering understanding. If you do this with and for each other, springtime will come again.

Lord, You are our strength, our shield, and our protection. As we go through losses and disappointments, help us to keep perspective, to persevere through the trials. Show us Yourself. Through Your Spirit help us to comfort each other. In Christ's name we pray, amen.

Losses

REFLECTION

"When we stand in the middle of a life storm, it seems as if the storm has become our way of life. We cannot see a way out. We are unable to chart a course back to smoother waters. We feel defeated—and broken. Will that brokenness produce a cynicism that will keep us forever in the mire of 'if only' thinking? Or will we yield up that brokenness to the resources of One who calms the winds and the waves, heals the brokenhearted, and forgives the most grievous of sins? The choice is ours."

Verdell Davis, *Riches Stored in Secret Places*

"A man may perform astonishing feats and comprehend a vast amount of knowledge, and yet have no understanding of himself. But suffering directs a man to look within. If it succeeds, then there, within him, is the beginning of his learning."

Søren Kierkegaard, quoted in *Secrets of Successful Humor*

LET'S TALK ABOUT IT

1 Talk about the different ways each of you responds to loss.

2 Commit to each other now, before a crisis or loss, that you will be there for each other, no matter what.

YOUR NOTES/REFLECTIONS/PRAYERS/GOALS

_____

_____

_____

_____

_____

_____

_____

_____

_____

_____

_____

_____

_____

_____

PRAYING FOR THE PRESENCE OF GOD IN OUR

STRESS

50

I am leaving you with a gift—peace of mind and heart. And the peace I give isn't

like the peace the world gives. So don't be troubled or afraid.

John 14:27

PRAYER

So much presses in on us, Lord. Bills to pay, appointments to keep, kids to raise, expectations to meet. Teach us, Lord, how to deal with the pressures of life. Help us resist the temptation of saying yes to the wrong things, and remind us to come away and be still with You. May we live by Your agenda, not the agenda of the hectic world around us. Amen.

SCRIPTURE

"Pity me, O Lord, for I am weak. . . . and I am upset and disturbed. My mind is filled with apprehension and with gloom. Oh, restore me soon" (Ps. 6:2-3, TLB).

As Nancie and I look back over our marriage, the things that we thought were marriage problems were more often personal problems that were exacerbated by stress. Health problems, financial difficulties, overcrowded schedules, challenges at work, our children's lives, and a thousand other things can create stress in our marriage. Stress can drive us apart, tear at our marriage. They can also bring us closer, if we allow them to. I'm convinced that much of what stresses our lives deeply affects the marriage.

Shirley and John have been living with two very stressful situations: raising a handicapped child (now nearly thirty years old) and running a family business. They have learned that it is absolutely essential for them to get away now and then because if they do not, they are completely drained and have nothing left for each other. Shirley said, "One weekend away from home totally renews our relationship, and we are different people. But we have found we must do this to survive."

Life is expendable, like a bank account, says Hans Selye, author of *The Stress of Life*. When one keeps adding stressors (expenditures)—without making deposits, one eventually runs in the red. According to Dr. Selye, it is a matter of addition and subtraction. We become overstressed when we have an overload and not enough time and balance to relax.

Therapist Delores Curran conducted research among families, charting their stress levels. In her report, *Stress and the Healthy Family,* she indicates that highly stressed people show specific symptoms:

- A constant sense of urgency, no time to release and relax
- Underlying tension that causes sharp words and misunderstandings
- A mania to escape—to one's room, car, or garage
- A nagging desire for a simpler life
- A lack of "me" or "couple" time
- Guilt for not being and doing everything for all the people in our lives

Curran goes on to point out that highly stressed people tend to seek a place to lay blame (job, school, etc.), while what she calls "stress-effective people" tend to seek solutions (budgeting time or prioritizing activities).

Not all stress is bad. We need a certain amount just to keep us on our toes and to add challenge to life. And stress is very personal. What may be relaxing to one person may be stressful to another.

What is important in marriage is to recognize how stress influences a marriage. Stress often produces tension. It sometimes puts people on edge. It can cause depression and/or anxiety. It can produce sexual impotency. Release of stress can be done through anger, often pointed at an innocent person who is not even the cause of the stress. When looking at these outcomes of stress, it is easy to see why we need to make some effort to reduce our stress in healthy ways. Here are some suggestions:

Find the cause of your stress, and make an effort to change it. If your job is causing excessive stress, confront the problems at work and seek resolution. If that is not possible, change jobs. If your health is causing stress, seek help either to get well or discover ways to manage your illness. If conflict is causing stress, seek resolution, even if it requires counseling or a third party. When you identify the cause of your stress, you can find ways to deal with it.

Find healthy ways to release stress. Exercise helps to reduce stress. Getting away together for mini retreats or vacations is helpful. Making love can be helpful. Proper diet can be helpful. Prayer is extremely helpful. Talking it out with someone you trust is helpful. All of these are things couples can do with and for each other to help relieve stress.

Let Jesus be Lord. You may find this a bit trite, but it is true: If we commit our way to God, He will direct our path and even give us the desire of our heart. We know that it is easier said than done, but when we daily make the effort to commit our way to the Lord, He is faithful to interact in our daily affairs, provide guidance, and give us wisdom in making right choices and decisions. We make Him Lord daily through praying and meditating in silence to hear Him speak to us, reading His Word for guidance, and submitting our will in obedience to Him when we know what He wants us to do.

Lord, we want to be free from this sense of being overwhelmed, from feeling that we cannot cope with our life and situations. Give us wisdom about what to do to relieve the unhealthy stress we feel, and give us the power to trust You. Help us to slow down, not to strive so much. Help us to find time to be with You and with each other. Amen.

REFLECTION

"Most couples contend with some trait or circumstance that won't seem to go away, no matter what they do. Courage calls us to accept the malady, as Paul did his mysterious affliction, and lean hard on God's grace for the strength to endure what we neither deserve nor entirely welcome."

Diane Eble, article in *Marriage Partnership*

"Christianity is Christ living in us, and Christ has conquered everything. . . .
his is our great inheritance . . . this grip of clean love that holds us so fast that it keeps us
eternally free. This love, this life, this presence, is the witness that the spirit of Christ lives in us,
and that we belong to Him, and that the Father has given us to Him,
and no man shall snatch us out of His hand."

Thomas Merton, *No Man Is an Island*

LET'S TALK ABOUT IT

1 What is causing stress in your life, in your marriage?

2 What can you do to relieve that stress? Counseling? Confrontation? A change of environment? A totally new approach? More consistent prayer and listening to God? More physical exercise?

YOUR NOTES/REFLECTIONS/PRAYERS/GOALS

_____

_____

_____

_____

_____

Stress

PRAYING FOR THE PRESENCE OF GOD IN OUR

VALLEY TIMES

51

I may walk through valleys as dark as death but I won't be afraid. You are with

me, and your shepherd's rod makes me feel safe.

Psalm 23:4, CEV

PRAYER

Lord, life inevitably takes us through valleys of discouragement, either individually or together. Father, in these times, may we keep our focus on You. Help us view life from Your eternal perspective. Help us to remember that You will never forsake us and that You know exactly what we face. Thank You that we can hold on to You. Amen.

SCRIPTURE

"Come, O Lord, and make me well. In your kindness save me. . . . I am worn out with pain; every night my pillow is wet with tears. My eyes are growing old and dim with grief" (Ps. 6:4-7, TLB).

INSIGHT

I remember a time in our marriage when I was not sure we were going to make it. Nancie had been sick for months. She had been diagnosed with systemic lupus erythmetosis. Pain and depression became the biggest part of her world. I am the kind of guy who likes to fix things, including illnesses. I am impatient. So I wanted answers from Nancie and her doctors. None of the vague we-just-don't-know-for-sure stuff. I wanted a solid diagnosis, the right medicine, and the right diet. I wanted to fix it—now. My frustration and impatience only made matters worse.

It wasn't long before my frustration turned into a form of avoidance. Rather than get into the middle of Nancie's pain and depression, I began spending more hours at the office. I talked less with my wife. Knowing that I couldn't fix whatever was wrong with Nancie, I decided that talking about it would just make it worse. But avoidance only added to the problem. In addition to the pain and depression she was already facing, I had added a sense of isolation and loneliness. This went on for nearly four years.

Finally, things seemed so hopeless that it was difficult even to pray. It was at that point of desperation that we shared our burden with the little congregation at our local church. They diligently began to pray. Then a friend suggested that Nancie make a visit to Mayo Clinic. When the doctors at the clinic discovered that she did not have lupus, they took her off all her medication, and she began to improve almost immediately.

I can look back now and see the mistakes I made, but at the time of this valley experience, it was difficult to see anything of hope. If your marriage has not been in the valley yet, chances are it will be there sooner or later. You may be able to benefit from the lessons I learned.

Be patient. We live in a culture that is used to instant everything. But some things will not go away with the snap of our fingers. God often uses the valley to shape our character and to prove His faithfulness. It is wise for us to spend valley times holding on to God . . . waiting. The psalmist said, "Don't be impatient. Wait for the Lord, and he will come and save you! Be brave, stouthearted, and courageous. Yes, wait and he will help you" (Ps. 27:14, TLB).

Show compassion. When our spouse is going through a valley time, it doesn't do any good to tell him or her to snap out of it. Having compassion means identifying with our spouse's pain and suffering. It means we understand. "Try to show as much compassion as your Father does" (Luke 6:36, TLB).

Stay connected. When you stay connected to your spouse in valley times, you are really saying, "I am here for you. I will be with you throughout this storm. I will not abandon you physically or emotionally while you go through this situation." Using avoidance as a coping method during times of crisis is selfish. It may protect you from riding an emotional roller coaster for a time, but it leaves your spouse alone and feeling abandoned. By staying connected, the bond between you will deepen. And you can be a source of protection and encouragement.

William Booth, the founder of the Salvation Army, went through a time of discouragement early in his ministry. Nothing seemed to be going well for him: his preaching wasn't right, and he was criticized for his lack of education. He was ready to quit. But his wife and coworker, Catherine, stayed in there with him. She gave him this wonderfully encouraging advice: "Never mind who frowns if God smiles."

Keep Jesus in your boat. The Gospels tell the story about the disciples facing a storm at sea. Jesus was in the back of the boat, sleeping. It seemed as if all was going to be lost. As a last-ditch effort they awakened Jesus and shouted, "Lord, save us! We're sinking!" (Matt. 8:25, TLB). Jesus simply said to the storm, "Be still," and the storm evaporated. God promises to carry us through the storms of life if we will let Him. It's a good idea to keep Jesus in your boat so that when the time comes, you, too, can say, "Lord, save us! We're sinking!"

If you are the one going through the valley, remember that God—not your spouse—is your source. The temptation is to expect our husband or wife to fill up all the holes, to meet all our needs. It is an impossible thing to ask of one another. Only God can fill up these holes. Only God can be God to us.

Lord, we know that the valley times will come. Give us courage and compassion to stand together, to trust You. Lord, thank You for promising to be in our boat. Amen.

REFLECTION

"There is comfort in the strength of love; t'will make a thing endurable which else would overset the brain, or break the heart."

William Wordsworth, quoted in *Quiet Moments for Couples*

"Between the shallow faith and the profound, between the faith of tradition and conviction, comes so often doubt . . . [and] between the seasons comes the equinoctial storm. The old traditional faith is shaken with the wind of doubt. The tempest lasts through a long night, perhaps, before the morning dawns in sunshine, and the soul knows what it believes and why, and is filled with the energy and peace of the deeper faith."

Phillips Brooks, quoted in *Treasury of the Christian Faith*

LET'S TALK ABOUT IT

1 How do you handle your valley times? What do you need from each other?

2 Most marriage vows include "for better, for worse." Are you prepared to tough it out if it is "for worse"? Can you recommit to those vows to each other today?

YOUR NOTES/REFLECTIONS/PRAYERS/GOALS

_____

_____

_____

_____

_____

_____

_____

_____

_____

_____

Valley Times

PRAYING FOR THE PRESENCE OF GOD IN OUR

SEASONS

52

To everything there is a season, a time for every purpose under heaven.

Ecclesiastes 3:1, NKJV

PRAYER

Thank You, God, for change. How boring life would be without life's seasons and variety. While I welcome change when it seems to fit what I want, I confess that at times I resist the changes that cause me to rethink my prejudices or cause me loss. Help me accept the seasons of leaving, losing, and maturity. Help me to welcome Your will for my life with an open heart. Amen.

SCRIPTURE

"But the godly will flourish like palm trees and grow strong like the cedars of Lebanon. For they are transplanted into the Lord's own house. They flourish in the courts of our God. Even in old age they will still produce fruit; they will remain vital and green" (Ps. 92:12-14).

INSIGHT

I love seeing couples who have been together for fifty years or more. Their lives speak of commitment that makes me know it is possible to love someone through thick and thin, for a long, long time. I know of a couple who has stayed married for sixty years. They were married just after the Great Depression. She was sixteen, and he was twenty-six. He was told that she was much too young, that he was robbing the cradle. She probably was too young. She had her first child when she was eighteen. I marvel that they made it.

They have been through a lot of life together—post-depression days, World War II, fires, accidents, surgeries, near bankruptcy, and family deaths. They have logged many miles, sometimes moving from state to state looking for work, and even living once in a tent.

Seasons

They speak now of the many good times together. They have no remorse about the relationship or the life they have lived. They take pride in their children and grandchildren. I notice they often look at each other in very caring ways and frequently speak in tones of understanding and gentleness.

I know these people well. They are my parents, Harold and Betty Carmichael, and I have been able to observe this union from the inside. Harold and Betty's love is committed love that has lasted through the many seasons of life. Because of them, I know it is possible

to survive all of the seasons of life and make it through.

When Nancie married me, she thought she had married a guy who was headed toward being a pastor (at least that's what I intended to do), who would live in the same community for thirty years (much as Nancie had done growing up in the same house, the same church). Of course, I thought I had married a starry-eyed blonde who would throw every energy into homemaking (much like my mother, who is the grand-champion apple pie baker of Santa Cruz County!). Nancie didn't know she had married a risk taker who would drag her with him through several occupational variations and geographical locations. And I certainly didn't know I had married an independent, analytical woman driven to write.

These surprises have led us on a roller coaster for more than thirty years. Sometimes the ride was very exciting. Other times we've landed with a thud. We have had our ideals crushed, our dreams rearranged. We have also seen the hand of God in making something of our efforts.

Life changes for all of us. We go through seasons: the newlywed years, the "gathering years" (gathering careers, homes, kids, etc.), the middle-age years, the "sending years" (sending kids off to college, into marriage) with the accompanying empty nest, the

224

grandparenting years, and the senior-citizen years. Each of these seasons affects our marriage.

Other seasons can also affect life greatly. Divorce, death, prolonged illness, financial reversals, emotional heartaches, and a variety of other major hitches in the road can shape our marriages.

But it is important to remember that both the good and the bad usually last only for a season. When our first two children were in diapers, Nancie and I thought that season would never end. Now we look back and wonder how that season flew by so rapidly. We lived and acted as if our kids would be at our dinner table forever.

The important thing for us to do in the seasons of life is to remember how fleeting all of life really is. It is imperative that we *live* in the place we find ourselves now. If you constantly plan and live for a future time, you will miss the life you now have. It is also important to invest in your marriage now.

Neglect is one of the great sins of failed marriages. Give to each other what is needed now so that the relationship will grow with time. It is also important to recognize that whatever you are going through now, whether good or bad, will not last forever. When we embrace the seasons of life together, somehow the journey is much sweeter. To say we went through life together and made it in spite of the surprises is an awesome thing, and I believe it pleases God.

Staying in love and growing in love take a lot of courage, humility, and commitment. The foundation that holds all of us in marriage is our commitment to our marriage and the commitment to follow Christ into and through every season, no matter what.

Lord, help us to embrace the seasons of our lives with acceptance and anticipation. Help us to accept our own mortality. Help us to take each day and invest it wisely, with Your blessing. Defeat fear and doubt by giving us courage and hope. In Jesus' name, amen.

REFLECTION

"There is nothing more lovely in life than the union of two people whose love for one another has grown through the years from the small acorn of passion into a great rooted tree. Surviving all vicissitudes, and rich with its manifold branches, every leaf holding its own significance."
Vita Sackville-West, quoted in *Speaking of Marriage*

"It is love in old age, no longer blind, that is true love. For love's highest intensity doesn't necessarily mean its highest quality. . . . Passersby commonly see little beauty in the embrace of young lovers on a park bench, but the understanding smile of an old wife to her husband is one of the loveliest things in the world."

Booth Tarkington, quoted in *Quiet Moments for Couples*

LET'S TALK ABOUT IT

1 What season of life are you in right now? How are you maximizing the opportunities and circumstances that this season presents?

2 What are you doing to prepare your marriage for the next season?

YOUR NOTES/REFLECTIONS/PRAYERS/GOALS

_____

_____

_____

_____

_____

_____

_____

_____

_____

_____

_____

Seasons

Our Keepsake Page

A PLACE TO REFLECT, MEASURE OUR PROGRESS, AND SET NEW GOALS

Great and marvelous are your actions, Lord God Almighty.

Revelation 15:3

_____
DATE

THIS IS THE _____ YEAR OF OUR MARRIAGE AND THE _____ YEAR WE HAVE BEEN USING THIS BOOK.

As we look back through the chapters of this book, how has God been working in our marriage, and how have we responded? _____

_____

_____

What are the new challenges we have faced this past year, and how is God helping us meet those challenges? _____

_____

_____

What are the specific things we plan to pray for in the coming year regarding our marriage?

_____

_____

_____

_____

Our Keepsake Page

God is our refuge and strength.

Psalm 46:1

_____
DATE

THIS IS THE _____ YEAR OF OUR MARRIAGE AND THE _____ YEAR WE HAVE BEEN USING THIS BOOK.

As we look back through the chapters of this book, how has God been working in our marriage, and how have we responded? _____

_____

_____

What are the new challenges we have faced this past year, and how is God helping us meet those challenges?_____

_____

_____

What are the specific things we plan to pray for in the coming year regarding our marriage?

_____

_____

_____

_____

Our Keepsake Page

A PLACE TO REFLECT, MEASURE OUR PROGRESS, AND SET NEW GOALS

Dear children, let us stop just saying we love each other; let us really show it by our actions.

1 John 3:18

_____
DATE

THIS IS THE _____ YEAR OF OUR MARRIAGE AND THE _____ YEAR WE HAVE BEEN USING THIS BOOK.

As we look back through the chapters of this book, how has God been working in our marriage, and how have we responded? _____

_____

_____

What are the new challenges we have faced this past year, and how is God helping us meet those challenges? _____

_____

_____

What are the specific things we plan to pray for in the coming year regarding our marriage?

_____

_____

_____

_____

Our Keepsake Page

A PLACE TO REFLECT, MEASURE OUR PROGRESS, AND SET NEW GOALS

Trials are only to test your faith, to see whether or not it is strong and pure.

1 Peter 1:7, TLB

_____
DATE

THIS IS THE _____ YEAR OF OUR MARRIAGE AND THE _____ YEAR WE HAVE BEEN USING THIS BOOK.

As we look back through the chapters of this book, how has God been working in our marriage, and

how have we responded? _____

_____

_____

What are the new challenges we have faced this past year, and how is God helping us meet those

challenges?_____

_____

_____

What are the specific things we plan to pray for in the coming year regarding our marriage?

_____

_____

_____

_____

Our Keepsake Page

A PLACE TO REFLECT, MEASURE OUR PROGRESS, AND SET NEW GOALS

Once I was young, and now I am old. Yet I have never seen the godly forsaken,

nor seen their children begging for bread.

Psalm 37:25

_____
DATE

THIS IS THE _____ YEAR OF OUR MARRIAGE AND THE _____ YEAR WE HAVE BEEN USING THIS BOOK.

As we look back through the chapters of this book, how has God been working in our marriage, and

how have we responded? _____

_____

_____

What are the new challenges we have faced this past year, and how is God helping us meet those

challenges?_____

_____

_____

What are the specific things we plan to pray for in the coming year regarding our marriage?

_____

_____

_____

Bill and Nancie Carmichael are the former publishers of *Virtue* and *Christian Parenting Today* magazines, and Nancie is the editor-at-large of *Virtue*. Their commitment to strengthening marriages and families takes them throughout the country as they conduct "Habits of a Healthy Home" seminars. In addition to three other books they have written together—*Lord, Bless My Child, The Best Things Ever Said about Parenting,* and *601 Quotes about Marriage and Family*—Bill has written *Habits of a Healthy Home,* and Nancie has written *Your Life, God's Home.*

Bill and Nancie, who have been married for over thirty years, have a deep desire to help couples grow in their relationship to God and to each other. The Carmichaels live in Sisters, Oregon, where they enjoy walking together in the beautiful Three Sisters mountain area. They are the parents of five children and the grandparents of one grandson.